NIGHTMARE IN NAPA

NIGHTMARE IN NAPA

THE WINE COUNTRY MURDERS

PAUL LaRosa

POCKET STAR BOOKS
New York   London   Toronto   Sydney

Pocket Star Books
A Division of Simon & Schuster, Inc.
1230 Avenue of the Americas
New York, NY 10020

Copyright © 2007 by CBS Broadcasting Inc.
All rights reserved. *48 Hours Mystery* and related marks are trademarks of CBS Broadcasting Inc.

First Pocket Star Books paperback edition May 2007

POCKET STAR and colophon are registered trademarks of Simon & Schuster, Inc.

Manufactured in the United States of America

10 9 8 7 6 5 4 3 2 1

ISBN-13: 978-1-4165-4365-7
ISBN-10:   1-4165-4365-1

Cover design by Anna Dorfman

For information about special discounts for bulk purchases, please contact Simon & Schuster Special Sales at 1-800-456-6798 or business@simonandschuster.com.

For Alex and Peter

FOREWORD

An Explanatory Note

This book is the first in a series to be based on the broadcasts of the CBS News magazine *48 Hours Mystery*. Because this book draws on the work of my colleagues, I have to acknowledge that it would not have been possible without the reporting skills of my fellow producers. In producing any hour for *48 Hours Mystery*, producers typically will supervise the videotaping of more than one hundred hours of interviews and other material. All of those hours are edited down to make a compelling, fast-moving, one-hour broadcast for prime-time television. This should give you an idea of the wealth and breadth of material we compile for each broadcast. Because of time restrictions, a lot of material never makes it onto the air. So much is left out that, well, you could write a book, and that's just what we're going to do in this series.

I've been able to use much of the fascinating material that never gets aired. That's why I am so indebted to the producers who spent months interviewing and putting together the story of Adriane Insogna and Leslie Mazzara, two special young women. I did additional reporting for this book and traveled to the Napa Valley and Florida to meet face-to-face with many of the principals and their families, friends, cops, locals, and lawyers. With some of those involved, I developed an e-mail relationship; some I spoke to by phone. There were, as there always are, some people who refused to speak with me for the book.

Most of the quotes in this book are taken from videotaped and transcribed interviews done by *48 Hours* producers and correspondent Bill Lagattuta; the rest come from my own reporting. There were some sources who asked not to be named or acknowledged. In a few instances, minor incidental conversations have been recreated, but only when participants recounted exactly what had happened. A handful of names have been changed, but all names of principals remain true.

Special thanks to my talented colleagues Susan Zirinsky and Al Briganti for their vision; Peter Schweitzer for his patient guidance; Abra Potkin, Patti Aronofsky, Joanna Cetera, Sue McHugh, and John DiTarsio for their generosity and memories; to Josh Gelman for his understanding; to Mead Stone for his great editing; to Bill Lagattuta for his intelligent and incisive questioning. I am grateful to my friends Melissa Sanford, Marc Goldbaum, Allen Alter, and Alec Sirken for listening to me rattle on and on about this project. And a word of thanks to intern Monika Blackwell, who came to CBS to work in television and found herself working on a book, always with eagerness. To my mother, Lucy; my sister, Karen; and my brother, Bob, for their support.

Finally, this book and my work would not be possible without the love and good humor (read: they laugh at my jokes) of my wife, Susan, and my children, Alexandra and Peter.

Contents

PART TWO

The Investigation

PART THREE

The Confession

INTRODUCTION

The Two Napas

When the painful reality set in, when those living in the city of Napa truly understood what had happened that Halloween night of 2004—that an unnamed intruder had broken into a home in their quiet little town and murdered two defenseless young women—residents were left almost speechless. Mayor Ed Henderson sums up the feelings of many when he says: "Bad things happen in paradise, and we live in paradise. I am so sorry that this has happened."

Todd Shulman, a detective with the Napa City Police Department, agrees: "This has robbed a lot of people of the sense of security they have. People are searching for a reason why this happened. I've talked to some longtime cops who've been here for thirty years and they think this is the most violent crime they've ever seen here. It's a once-in-a-career type thing."

How in the world could something like this—a vicious double murder reflective of the darkest, most base elements of human behavior—happen in a place dedicated to the good life? "This isn't supposed to happen in Napa," says Marsha Dorgan, a longtime reporter for the *Napa Valley Register*. "It's safe here, you know? We're not Oakland. We're not Vallejo, we're not even American Canyon, which is just south of us. People here feel safe, and I think now people feel violated. Besides being afraid, people were violated because this is not supposed to happen in Napa."

But it is a cliché to say that Napa is the type of place where murder doesn't happen. In twenty-first-century America, murder occurs everywhere and that old saw cannot be trotted out every time something horrific happens in a small town. And Napa, make no mistake, is a small town with a population of only about 70,000 people. Crime does occur in Napa—even murder (the last murder had occurred in 2001)—but before Adriane and Leslie were murdered, twin killings were exceptional. "I've been here twenty years, and I can't think of a double homicide we've had," says Commander Jeff Troendly, who is the public voice of the Napa City Police Department.

Marsha Dorgan begs to differ but only slightly. She says the last double homicide was in 1999 but agrees with Troendly that Napa has a very low crime rate and most Napans don't give it a second thought. It's just not what everyday life is all about. In Napa, many people—and this is a reality, not just a cliché—do not lock the doors on their homes or their cars. People feel connected to each other because they are connected: your next-door neighbor could be your sister's ex-boyfriend or your mother's best friend's daughter. And then there is the glorious weather—some eight months of sunshine—and the picturesque countryside.

"Napa is a beautiful place to live," says Dorgan. "It's got vineyards. It's got hotels. It's got upscale restaurants. . . . We get tourists from all over the world who come here and they come to sample the wines and ride the wine train. We've got those hot air balloons, and it's really quite a tourist place, but the people who live here don't think of it like that. This is just where we live, where we work, and it's a very small community in a lot of ways."

Dorgan is onto something, the dichotomy between what Napa actually is and what we think it is. There really are two Napas: "tourist Napa"—the one that exists in our collective virtual memory—and then the "real Napa." For those who live there, Napa is a small, former blue-collar and agricultural town trying to cope with an influx of very big money and highbrow pretensions. "Napa is the anchor for the Valley," says Shulman. "The workers who work in the fields live here, and it still has a small-town feel to it. You meet people you know all the time in the stores. It has a great farmer's market on Wednesday when they close down part of downtown and sell crafts and food. It has the same feel to it that it had thirty years ago."

As Shulman knows, it wasn't so very long ago that Napa was known more for its prunes than its wine, back when the largest employers were Kaiser Steel and Napa State Hospital, a psychiatric facility. "There are still a lot of old-timers here who hate the things that are going on," says Jeff Schectman of KVON radio.

These longtime and native Napans are not nearly as impressed by the local sights that draw visitors from all over the world. It reminds one of blue-collar native New Yorkers who would rather rush home to mundane neighborhoods like Maspeth, Queens, and Bay Ridge, Brooklyn, rather than spend one extra second in "the city" to attend what they consider an overpriced and overpraised Broadway play. One local Napa cop, forced by his wife to ride the fabled wine train with another couple, groans when he recalls how bored he was: "You've seen one vine, you've seen them all."

And there's something else about Napa. "There are only a couple of ways in and out of the Valley," Shulman says, noting how that has prevented a lot of crime from sweeping into his adopted city. Napa still exists in its own bubble, not unlike Savannah, Georgia. It's not totally isolated, just a bit off the beaten path. It's not an exit off I-80 but tucked away on Highway 29. It's always been only forty-eight miles away from San Francisco, but it's always seemed much farther. But that is changing. These days, folks actually live in San Francisco and commute to work in Napa because it's a reverse commute; that used to be unheard of. And the real Napa, while still surrounded by natural beauty, has a downtown core that is exceedingly average. Yes, it's nicer than, say, Akron, but that's not saying a lot.

Take a look for yourself. There are some cute Victorian gingerbread homes, but at Napa's center is one of those fake pedestrian malls that don't really work. There are some forlorn-looking stores and even some abandoned storefronts begging for attention. Tourists who find themselves there accidentally because they've heard so much of "tourist Napa" wander around streets looking at stores like Cribs and Bibs and the Doll House and wonder what all the fuss is about. Most big suburban malls have better stores and are twice as glamorous. In fairness, there are pockets of charm, restaurants like Angele's on the water or Uva's, but the overall picture is not what you think. It is a town of poorly designed parking lots that sometimes force you to back up into oncoming traffic and a place where rumors that Whole Foods may open a store spark a fair amount of conversation.

Napa is a former blue-collar city coming to grips with gentrification, and it's not all that pretty. Schectman puts it more bluntly: "Downtown Napa is utterly without charm."

But just say the word *Napa* to outsiders and watch the smiles. Maybe they were there once and visited a winery, had some wine, ate a great meal, took a mud bath, had a massage. Even if they were never there, they still smile, because they imagine doing all those things in Napa.

The publicity machine has done its job so wonderfully that there is nary a bad thought associated with the place whether you've been there or not, whether you like wine or not. In the 1980s, Napa was the setting for the prime-time soap opera *Falcon Crest*; the television family's palatial home in the opening shot is actually the old Spring Mountain Winery. Or perhaps the city brings to mind the popular film *Sideways*, which, by the way, did not take place in Napa but in the wine country north of Santa Barbara. Few people know that, and Napa has gotten the residual goodwill that another region can stake as its own. It's amazing, really; Napa is kind of like ice cream but better. In our imaginations, the city is swell, and, unlike ice cream, it doesn't have any calories.

So here's the truth: what most of us think of as glorious Napa is actually the *Napa Valley*. You know that picture you have in your head of the to-die-for town lined with comely little storefronts? What you're thinking of can be found in St. Helena, which has a main street as charming as a storybook, or perhaps it's Calistoga, which has its own version of the perfect western main street. Wake up in an inn or hotel in one of those Up Valley towns, look out your window to see hot air balloons magically suspended above breathtaking vistas, and you'll swear you're in the American Eden, as some have called the Napa Valley.

But that is not the city of Napa, where the murders of Adriane Insogna and Leslie Mazzara took place, the city that was suddenly gripped by fear, courtesy of an unknown killer who was ruthless and, so far, undetectable.

PART ONE

The Victims

ONE

The Scariest Night of the Year

By 7:00 p.m. on Halloween night, 2004, Lauren Meanza was back home at 2631 Dorset Street in Napa, California. It had been a busy Sunday. She had played some soccer—a game she loved—and then spent the rest of the day doing something she found not nearly as enjoyable: shopping. The shopping had been more exhausting than the soccer, and Lauren was happy to be home. Greeting her as she pulled her car into the garage was the effigy of a luckless witch hanging from the front porch to let the local children know that, yes, this was a Halloween house where trick-or-treaters were more than welcome.

And they were. Lauren's two roommates,

Adriane Insogna and Leslie Mazzara, were there at the front door, giggling, cooing, and feigning fright at the little ghosts and goblins coming to call in sometimes spooky, but mostly sweet, costumes. The house supply of candy was going fast, but Adriane and Leslie didn't mind; they couldn't hand it out fast enough.

Lauren wasn't quite as enthusiastic about the annual Halloween ritual. "It's not that I don't like kids or anything," she was quick to point out. Rather, it was that her aging dog, Chloe, a German shepherd mix, didn't like strangers coming to the door and let everyone know it by barking each and every time someone rang the bell. It cracked the roommates up, and they looked at Chloe and laughed every time the doorbell rang.

It was a fun night, as it often was down on Dorset Street, just minutes from Napa's downtown. Lauren, Adriane, and Leslie—three single women—got along famously and without "all that drama" that's part of many roommate situations. All three were brunettes and twenty-six years old, but that's where the similarities ended.

Leslie Mazzara, a small-town beauty queen with stunning green eyes, had been in Napa for only six months. She grew up near Orlando,

Florida, and later in Anderson, South Carolina, and went to college at the University of Georgia. Being a Southerner, Leslie was the most distinctive of the three roommates, simply because she was the outsider. New to town, Leslie was in a hurry to meet new people, and she did so with a vengeance. She was brimming with social energy, eating out, going to bars, and dancing till all hours of the night. Leslie loved dancing and had studied classical ballet for fifteen years. During the day, she worked at the Niebaum-Coppola winery in the sales department, where she used her well-honed people skills to good advantage.

Adriane Insogna (rhymes with *lasagna*) was an assistant engineer at the Napa Sanitation District, having graduated from Cal Poly down the coast in beautiful San Luis Obispo. She was local and had been raised Up Valley in Calistoga, where she'd lived since she was nine years old. Adriane was a bit overweight, with a warm smile and an engaging personality. She was close to her mother, Arlene Allen, and made an effort to include Arlene, who was twice divorced, in some of her social activities. In short, she was the perfect daughter. She couldn't cook, friends said, but she loved to bake, and she and Leslie had made Halloween cupcakes that very day. Adriane also loved volleyball and volunteered as a scorekeeper at Napa Valley Community College.

Lauren Meanza was the quietest of the roommates. If you had to rate the three and pick the one who was the least social, Lauren, who spoke unemotionally and affected a blasé attitude, would win hands down. A jock and the most athletic of the three, she coached volleyball at the local community college and played volleyball and soccer in adult leagues every chance she got. This was her first apartment on her own, and she had brought along her dog, Chloe. Lauren was also the neat freak of the three and often had to clean up after her buddies, but she didn't mind—not too much, anyway. They were both good roommates, kind and loving, and she knew they'd do anything for her.

Lauren had met Adriane earlier in the year when they both took a volleyball class at Napa Community College. At that point, Lauren was still living nearby with her parents, but she didn't know a lot of people in Napa. In fact, that's how she'd connected with Adriane, who had approached Lauren between games. Adriane knew a lot of people in the Valley, and as she prodded Lauren to see if they had any mutual acquaintances, Lauren finally blurted out, "I don't have any friends in Napa."

"Well, you do now," Adriane answered.

And so their friendship was formed. Back in February 2004, when Lauren found the little house for rent on Dorset Street and thought it would be a good place to live, Adriane was the first one she approached to be her roommate. Adriane was all for it, and with the help of her tight clique of friends—Ben Katz, Lily Prudhomme, and Lily's boyfriend, Eric Copple—she successfully moved her stuff into the compact house. From the beginning, there were fun times, beginning with the first night Lauren and Adriane hung out and had pizza and beer with Ben, Lily, and Eric. And it wasn't long before Lauren, who was breaking out of her quiet shell, introduced herself to a group of young women living in the house next door. They were a fun bunch, too, none more so than Leslie Mazzara. "She was a pistol," Lauren said, "She definitely was a Southern girl, with lots of makeup, and right away I really liked her. She was definitely different than I was, very girly-girl, lots of makeup and very feminine."

Leslie, with her sugar-coated accent and approachable personality, attracted men in droves, and they often fell hard for her. While there's no doubt she was very pretty, her real beauty seemed to spring from somewhere inside, and it was her charisma that brought people in. Friends say she had a way of connecting that was otherworldly; she effortlessly made every person she came across feel a solid connection to her. It was a gift and she had it long before she was ever a pageant winner. When Leslie's own housemates announced plans to move out, Lauren and Adriane asked her to move in with them. They both really enjoyed Leslie's vivacious personality, there was a spare upstairs bedroom, and the rent would be split three ways instead of just two. Leslie agreed and moved into the house in late June 2004.

It was now Halloween, and the girls were looking forward to Christmas, when Leslie promised to make Southern-style treats and show her new friends what a real, old-fashioned Christmas was all about. That was a point of friendly debate between Lauren and Leslie. Being from the South, Leslie told them she considered Californians to be too guarded, while Southerners were more open and friendly. Lauren found herself good-naturedly defending her California brethren.

By 9:00 p.m., the trick-or-treaters were winding down, and the women were settling in for the night. Even though it was Halloween, they had no plans to go to a party or a bar, because the next day, Monday, was a workday. Despite Napa's worldwide reputation as the capital of California's beauteous wine country, it is not, as any young adult resident will tell you, exactly party central. The girls had their favorite bars, such as the Bounty Hunter, Uva's, and Downtown Joe's, but most of the time, it was the same old faces, which was one reason Leslie attracted so much attention as the new girl in town. This particular Halloween, falling on a Sunday night, seemed more quiet than most, just another night to grab some food from the fridge and plop down in front of the television.

Adriane told the others she was going to pay a short visit to her on-again, off-again boyfriend, Christian Lee, who lived one block away. Lauren headed into the kitchen to fix something to eat while Leslie kept her company. Then they both moved into the living room. Lauren had a DVD set of the HBO series *Six Feet Under*, and they watched an episode and chatted until about 9:30 p.m., when Lauren got a phone call and wandered into her downstairs bedroom. About twenty-five minutes later, she heard Leslie say good night.

"Good night," Lauren answered. "See you tomorrow."

Upstairs, Leslie prepared for bed and received her second call that day from Lee Youngblood Sr., the father of an ex-boyfriend from South Carolina. Friends say it bothered Leslie that Lee Senior called so often, and she didn't take the call. It seemed as though he never had gotten over the breakup between Leslie and his son. According to one of Leslie's closest friends, Leslie broke up with Lee at least partly because of his father. She spent a lot of time with that family, and the more she got to know Lee's father, the less she was sure she wanted to be a part of it. Ultimately, she decided to part ways with Lee and leave South Carolina. That did not keep Lee Senior from calling.

By 10:30 p.m., Adriane was back from Christian's house and found Lauren back in front of the television.

"It's been a long day," Adriane said. "I'm going to bed. See you tomorrow."

"I'm turning in soon, too," Lauren said.

Adriane went straight upstairs to her bedroom, across a tiny second-floor landing from Leslie's room. The bathroom was between them. Inside her room, Adriane replayed the last twenty-four hours in her head. She had been with Christian the previous night and long into the morning hours and had gotten virtually no sleep. She was as close to love as she'd ever been. She was tired but happy and wanted to luxuriate in that feeling a bit longer, so before falling off, she sent Christian one last text message: "Thank you for yesterday. It was one of the best days ever. I wish it could be forever."

Downstairs, Lauren let her dog, Chloe, outside and closed up the house.

"I did the normal things," she said. "I checked to make sure all the doors were locked and secured and then went to bed about 11:00 p.m."

The house had a few ways to get in and out: the front door, the back door, and the garage door. "I made sure the back-door slider was locked because sometimes that would be left unlocked, but that night, I locked it."

She did not, however, check any of the windows, even though her bedroom was on the first floor.

She was tired, and by 11:30, she was asleep.

TWO

"Please, God, Help Me"

Sometime after 1:00 a.m., Lauren awoke to hear Chloe growling and barking. Chloe always slept in Lauren's room, and she looked over to find her old dog looking out the window that faced the back of the house. A motion detector had tripped a sensor light, illuminating the backyard. Was someone outside? Lauren dismissed the thought, figuring it was one of the local cats that had tripped the sensor before. "Quiet," she told Chloe, and pulled her back onto the bed.

The sensor light clicked off, and Lauren drifted back to sleep, but it wasn't long before she was awakened again. Now there was a noise coming from inside the house near the front door. In fact, Lauren thought it was the front door and that someone, probably a boyfriend of Leslie's, was there for a late-night "booty call." This, in fact, was a new development and had caused a bit of friction in the house. Lauren and Adriane were concerned about Leslie's late-night visitors. She was seeing two men regularly, and a recent incident had troubled her roommates. Just two days before, Leslie had brought some-one home, and the noise from their lovemak-ing kept everyone awake in a way that made the small house feel more claustrophobic than cozy. Leslie had apologized in an e-mail for "the late-night rumble," and the women had held a house meeting where they agreed that, yes, they might entertain men some nights. Now, Lauren thought, Leslie was wasting no time.

Chloe barked again, but again, Lauren pulled the dog back away from her bedroom door. She felt she was just being considerate, giving Leslie the benefit of the doubt. "I was trying to quiet Chloe down so she wouldn't wake up anybody," Lauren says. "I had her quiet down and go back to bed."

She listened a little more closely but didn't hear anyone climbing the wooden stairs, which were normally quite loud; perhaps she'd missed it when Chloe was barking. She tried to go back to sleep, but a noise in Leslie's bedroom—right above Lauren's room—brought her back. "I really need to get some rest," she thought. "I have to get up in the morning for work."

At that point, whoever had been in Leslie's room seemed to be going over to Adriane's room. The noise had shifted. "Now, *that's* odd," Lauren thought, but maybe Leslie's visitor needed to use the bathroom, located between the two second-floor bedrooms.

A moment later, a "bumping" noise was coming from Adriane's room. "It sounded like a bed up against a wall," she said. "It would bump a few times and it would stop. So then I thought, okay, Adriane's got a visitor, and that's going to keep me up. I just started thinking, kind of, it was, like, you know, sex. It was bumping against the wall, and so I started thinking, okay, I'm not going to be able to sleep again."

Now Lauren was almost fully awake and began to pay more attention, concentrating on the noise and where it was coming from.

The bumping stopped and then started up again. Lauren didn't want to be nosy, but she was curious. She was not in the mood to listen to someone else making love, but what could she do? "I stayed in bed and just listened," she said.

A few more minutes went by, and then there was a scream. Lauren could tell it was Adriane's voice. "There was a lot of commotion and a struggle. I was still thinking sex."

But then came a second scream, and the world tilted on its axis. "I knew it was a terror scream. There was terror, fear, in her voice. She just kept screaming. She wasn't saying anything at that point, but she was just screaming, and I could tell she was fighting or struggling with someone," Lauren said. "Things were being thrown around the room, and I could hear things falling over, and there's bumping into furniture. Just a lot of commotion. She had a lot of stuff in her room, so I knew a lot of stuff was being knocked around. She was making a noise kind of like fighting. I mean, when she's exerting energy, she just sounded like she was fighting someone.

"Her voice was very loud, and by the second scream, I knew it was danger, so I sat up and jumped out of bed, and Chloe jumped up also."

Lauren realized she was living her biggest fear: being attacked in her own home by an intruder. She desperately wanted to help Adriane, but self-preservation is a powerful draw, and Lauren worried the attacker might turn on her. She didn't know whether to stay inside her room or risk leaving it. She chose to step outside her bedroom. Lauren was practically at the foot of the stairs. "Frozen" with fear, she stood still and listened for thirty more seconds while her roommate struggled to fight off whoever was attacking her. There were no lights on downstairs or in the stairway—"just darkness"—but there was plenty of noise coming from the upstairs bedroom.

"I could hear Adriane's voice, and it was, like, 'oh, God,' and she's just screaming and fighting. I don't think she had enough time to say much, but she was just fighting someone off."

Lauren heard glass breaking. There was some kind of little glass candelabra on the second-floor landing. The intruder was coming down the stairs, right at her. She knew whoever it was was moving extremely fast, because she heard him taking the steps two or three at a time. The intruder was flying, but Lauren spun around and made it outside to the backyard patio. Fear shot through her as she realized she was trapped by a big fence. If the attacker came out the back way, as she feared, she had nowhere to go. She turned around and faced the back of the house, not knowing what she might do or could do, thoughts racing through her head faster than she could process them.

She steeled herself for whatever was to come, but then she caught a break.

"I could hear the person struggling to get out the window, because the blinds, were just flailing around. They're wooden blinds, so they were making noise."

Once the intruder got through the window, the night was still except for one horrible sound: Adriane crying out for help from inside the house. Lauren forced herself to go back inside and again stood at the foot of the stairs. Whatever had happened upstairs was so horrible that she couldn't make her feet move. "I was scared."

Adriane's voice cut through the night: "Please, God, help me. Please, somebody, help me. Help me."

"Adriane, are you okay?" Lauren called out.

"No."

Lauren ran to get the portable phone in the kitchen to call 911, but there was no dial tone. Someone had cut the lines to the house, or a phone was off the hook. Again, Lauren could hear Adriane moaning for help but she couldn't make herself face whatever it was the intruder had done. She called instead for Leslie to come help her, to help Adriane.

Leslie did not answer.

"No, it's Adriane."

"I know it's Adriane, but where's Leslie?"

She didn't answer.

Slowly, Lauren headed up the stairs. The house was mostly dark, but her eyes had adjusted, and she could see blood streaks on a wall. A light was on in Adriane's room, and Lauren spotted Adriane on the floor on the far side of the bed between the bed and the window. "I could see half her body. Her chest was up, and she was lying there. She was trying to still breathe."

Lauren felt her bare feet sliding on something and realized that she was slipping on blood, a lot of blood. She knelt down to Adriane, "but at that point she couldn't speak anymore."

She was completely focused on Adriane, trying to see where her wounds were, what was wrong with her, and how she could help her, but in her peripheral vision, she saw another body to her right—it was Leslie, lying facedown in a pile of clothing. Lauren knew she had to find a phone that worked, had to call for help. Leslie was not moving, but Adriane was still alive, gurgling in the most horrible way imaginable. Lauren ran back down the stairs and grabbed her cell phone, but she knew from experience that her cell service was poor in the house, so she went back into the backyard, oblivious to where the intruder had gone.

THREE

All Saints Day

Lauren dialed 911 and waited. She knew instinctively that dialing 911 on a cell instead of the house phone might cause the call to go somewhere other than the Napa police and she was right. The call was answered by a 911 operator with Central California Dispatch. The tension in Lauren's voice is obvious on the tape, but she holds it together, even when the operator seems somewhat incredulous, possibly because it was still Halloween night.

> *Operator:* This is 9-1-1 emergency. What are you reporting?
> *LM:* Oh, my God, we got attacked! 2631 Dorset Street. Please help!

Operator: What's your address?

LM: 2631 Dorset Street.

Operator: What city are you in?

LM: Napa.

Operator: And who attacked you?

LM: I don't know.

Operator: You don't know who attacked you? Is that your house?

LM: Yeah, it was upstairs. I don't know who it was. I'm downstairs. I don't know what happened.

Operator: Okay.

LM: Both of my roommates are hurt.

Operator: Okay. So did you come home to find that your roommates had been attacked?

LM: Please hurry, hurry!

Operator: Did you come home to find this, yes or no?

LM: No.

Operator: What is your name? And you gave an address of 2631 Dorset?

LM: Yes.

Operator: D-O-R-S-E—

LM: Napa.

Operator: I understand. D-O-R-S-E-T-T, is that correct? How many people are injured?

LM: Two upstairs. I think they're dying. I
 swear to God!

Operator: Ma'am, hang on, thank you.

But then the connection was lost. Lauren
couldn't stand being in the house for even another second. "I realized the person might come
back," she said. "I might be in danger, so then
I grabbed Chloe."

Her car was in the garage, but she had no
choice but to go in and get it. As she backed out
and drove away, she called 911 again.

Operator: 9-1-1.

LM: Hi, I just called. It's 2631 Dorset
 Street in Napa, California. My roommates are upstairs. I think they're
 dying, they were attacked, and something happened. . . . I don't know if
 this guy's coming back.

Operator: Okay, I'm gonna put you on with
 Napa, so stay on the line, and I'll be
 right back with you, okay?

LM: Okay.

*(There is a series of beeps and ringing while the
call is rerouted.)*

Operator 3: Napa Emergency.

Operator: California central control transferring a caller from 2631 Dorset.

Operator 3: Okay, go ahead.

Operator: Go ahead.

LM: Yeah.

Operator 3: What happened? Yes, 2631 Dorset?

LM: Yeah.

Operator 3: Okay. Is it something I need an ambulance?

LM: Yes! Oh, my God. They're dying. I don't know what is going on. There is blood everywhere, and my roommate is gurgling.

Operator 3: Okay, so—

LM: I don't know what to do . . .

Operator 3: Wait, you're not back in the house?

LM: No. I got in my car and left. I don't know what to do. He jumped out of the window.

Operator 3: Who jumped out of the window?

LM: Somebody. I don't know. I was downstairs sleeping, and they're upstairs, and all of a sudden my roommate starts screaming.

Operator 3: Okay, who is bleeding?

LM: Both. My roommate, I don't know if

she's alive, one of 'em, and then the
other one—there's two of 'em in there.

Operator 3: Did you see any weapon?

LM: No, but they look like they were—I
didn't hear any guns, I don't know what
they did.

Operator 3: Okay. Can you go back towards
the house? You don't need to go inside. Can you just stay where you're
at? Can you just pull over to let me
know where . . . you need to just go to
a corner and tell me what corner.

LM: Okay. Sorry. I didn't want to sit around
there.

Operator 3: Okay, but you are helping them,
okay. You need to pull over and tell me
what intersection you're at.

LM: Okay.

Lauren turned her car around. She decided
she'd go back Dorset Street, but no way was she
pulling over until she saw the cops. She kept
driving back and forth, up and down her street
with her dog at her side, waiting for the police.
She kept talking to the operator.

Operator 3: Okay. I have help on the way for
your friends. Do you know what the per-

son looked like who jumped out the window? . . . Were you home when this happened?

LM: Yes, I was downstairs.

Operator 3: Okay. You pull over and tell me where you're at.

LM: Okay, I have to go back to the house. I'm driving away.

Operator 3: And you saw—what did the person look like?

LM: I didn't see anybody. I swear to you. I heard screaming, I heard screaming, and then I woke up, and I stayed where I was.

Operator 3: So you didn't actually see someone?

LM: No. I didn't see anybody.

Operator 3: Did you hear anything else?

LM: No. Oh, God.

Operator 3: Okay, so who are the people inside the house? What roommates, are they male, female?

LM: Two females upstairs.

Operator 3: And they were both bleeding?

LM: Yeah, well, one's unconscious on the ground, and then the other one's bleeding and gurgling. . . . I didn't know what to do.

Operator 3: Where was she bleeding from?

LM: I think her stomach. I didn't hear any shots . . .

Operator 3: Okay. Tell me—tell me where you're at. Where are you going?

LM: Kent and Dorset.

Operator 3: Kent and Dorset?

LM: Yeah, that's where my car is.

Operator 3: Okay, okay. Do you know who might have done this?

LM: No—no. I mean. No. I don't want to even speculate on that one.

Operator 3: Had you had any problems with anyone?

LM: No.

Operator 3: Okay. Just stay right there, okay?

LM: No. I really don't want to stop moving . . .

Operator 3: Well, I'm sorry, you said you didn't see anyone, and now you think he's on foot?

LM: Because I saw a broken window . . . and a guy jumping out of a window.

Operator 3: Okay, that's what I asked you. If you saw someone.

LM: I didn't see a guy . . .

Operator 3: Okay. You just saw a—a figure kind of thing.

LM: I heard a broken window. I went up to

go see how they were, they were upstairs. But I was downstairs. So I hear a
window that was broken. So somebody
jumped out of the window 'cause they
didn't know how to get out.

Operator 3: Okay, where was this window that
got broken?

LM: . . . in the kitchen downstairs.

Operator 3: Okay, so you're just—you're kinda
just thinking that someone jumped out.
But you didn't see anybody.

Lauren kept looking at the now haunted
house at 2631 Dorset each time she passed it.
The entire attack had taken but four minutes.
The house that had been so full of life just hours
before now was silent. The only movement came
from the effigy of the hanging witch, moving
slightly with the night breeze.

Halloween was over; it was November 1, All
Saints Day, and her roommates had moved on
to their eternal reward.

In Mexico, the holiday is known as the Day
of the Dead.

FOUR

No Pulse

Officer Darlene Elia was working the graveyard shift, the overnight, and she was parked where she usually sat on long overnights: in the parking lot of Napa High School at Jefferson and Lincoln. The major crimes in Napa tended to be DUIs and drug cases, and even those were sporadic; it was a quiet town for a cop, mostly. There had not been even a single murder so far in 2004, and the year was nearing its end.

But then came the call she'd never forget; there was a problem in a house on Dorset Street.

"Report of a 9-1-1 hang-up call. Problem unknown."

It was that first call from Lauren where her

cell phone had gone out before she could tell the operator what was happening. Still, the 911 computer had recorded the address as 2631 Dorset, and Officer Elia drove that way.

Within five minutes, dispatch called again. "The caller called back and says she and her roommates are being attacked by unknown intruder and there is blood everywhere."

Elia was now on high alert. She knew the neighborhood as a quiet residential subdivision where mostly families lived. With no traffic to speak of, she got there quickly and pulled up to the house. She could see Lauren waving down another police car coming from the opposite way. It was Sergeant Pat Manzer. Elia and he got out of their cars at the same time. Lauren was yelling and crying, "Oh, God! Oh, God!"

It was now 2:13 a.m.

The garage door was open, and there was a light on in the upstairs bedroom facing the street. Elia immediately noticed that the ground-floor window facing the street had some wooden blinds hanging out of it, as though someone had climbed out from the inside. A plant stand underneath the window had been knocked over, and a broken potted plant was on the ground.

Elia and Manzer tried to quiet Lauren down and get information about what was going on inside the house. They knew there was an in-truder, but they didn't know—and neither did Lauren—where he was, so the cops waited for backup, which arrived almost immediately. They all listened intently to see if they could hear any-thing or anyone inside the house, but all was quiet.

When the backup officers arrived, Elia and three others with guns drawn entered the house through the garage door that led into the kitchen. Immediately, Elia spotted a bunch of black plastic zip ties held together with a rubber band right beneath the window. It was the first clue. The ties were the sturdy type that could bind someone's hands and feet; cops sometimes use them as temporary handcuffs when they have to arrest a lot of people. Despite Lauren's reports of her roommates in distress, the cops moved purposefully up the stairs, unsure if the intruder might still be inside.

As she walked up the stairs, Elia instinctively knew she was on the verge of seeing something she'd never seen before. This had the feel of a horror house, as though something or someone might jump out from around a corner at any moment. This was something Elia had seen in movies, and suddenly it was happening in real life, her life. Blood droplets and footprints were clearly visible on the stairs. The footprints, which were Lauren's, were headed down the stairs. On the small upstairs landing, "there was a large amount of blood pooled in different areas," Elia said.

She kept her eye on the bathroom as Officers Grant Campagna and Officer Frank Esser entered Leslie's room, the bedroom on the right. There appeared to be a blood trail running from the right bedroom to the one on the left, as though someone gravely injured had crawled or been dragged from one bedroom to the other.

"Clear!" Esser hollered, loud enough for all to hear.

Even though she did not enter that bedroom right away, Elia could see inside. "There was blood on the floor, and there was blood on the bed, on the edge of the bed," she said.

Elia led the way into Adriane's bedroom. The hallway light was on, and there was a light on in Adriane's bedroom, coming from a lamp on a nightstand. "Did not see anybody on the bed," Elia said. "Saw a substantial amount of clothing on the floor, and as I scanned the bedroom, I noticed that there was some blood on the wall over in the corner. I looked down on the floor, and I observed a victim lying on the floor."

It was Leslie Mazzara.

"I entered the room to make contact with the subject that I saw lying on the floor, and as I went down to check her, I noticed that there was another victim lying on the other side of the bed between the bed and the window," Elia said.

It was Adriane Insogna.

Elia told Officer Aaron Medina to check on Adriane while Elia checked Leslie. She gently placed her hand on Leslie's blood-covered back. There was no rise and fall, no telltale movement. She felt for a pulse, but there was none. Medina did the same for Adriane and the result was the same. Both women were dead; they were growing colder as their blood ceased pumping and was pooling beneath them. It seemed as though Adriane had lived longer, because in her hand was a portable phone, but records show that she did not have the strength to make a call. It was a heartbreaking moment to think of what this young woman had gone through and how she desperately tried to call for help.

At that point, the paramedics were on the scene, but only one of them was allowed upstairs to confirm the cops' findings that both young ladies were dead. No one else was allowed up, so as not to disturb the crime scene. As far as anyone could see, there was no obvious sign of a murder weapon on the premises.

* * *

By 2:30 a.m., Janet Lipsey arrived. Lipsey, a twenty-eight-year-veteran, is the police forensic specialist for the Napa Police Department.

She immediately went to work, analyzing, processing, and collecting the forensic evidence at the scene. She began taking photographs and documented what the other cops had seen upon arriving. Lipsey photographed the first-floor window with the wooden blinds leading out, the blood on those blinds, the zip ties under the window tied together with a rubber band, the bloody footprints on the stairs, the blood trail leading from Leslie's bedroom to Adriane's, the positions of the victims, the blood spatters and stains all over the bedrooms. Lipsey noticed all that, but, befitting her role, she then came upon something the other cops had not noticed.

In the backyard, outside the rear garage door, was a cigarette butt. She cataloged it as item JL-302. Then she found another cigarette butt in the gutter at the driveway in front of the house. She assigned it number JL-2. She marked both spots with small yellow cones to signify she'd picked up evidence there.

Would the butts be important to the case? Were they relevant, or had they been left there sometime before? Lipsey didn't know, but a good crime-scene investigator doesn't get paid to guess.

She gets paid to collect those small bits of evidence that otherwise would disappear in a day or two.

FIVE

A Smell You Never Forget

At 6:15 on the morning of November 1, Jeff Schectman, the affable and intellectual general manager and twice-a-day talk-show host of KVON radio, was driving to work. The KVON studios are on Foster Road, a residential area just blocks away from 2631 Dorset Street. Schectman, a former movie producer in Hollywood, had followed his current wife up to Napa some nine years before when she was just a girlfriend, and he had never regretted his choice—neither the locale nor the wife. Schectman had seen his share of big-time action and immediately spotted the police cars and lights as he drove by Dorset Street.

He knew a big story when he saw one. He

pulled his car over, took out his press card, and walked up to the cop who was keeping people from driving down Dorset Street; crime-scene tape was cutting off both sides of the street.

"What's going on?" Schectman asked.

The cop said he wasn't supposed to say anything, but he told Schectman what he'd heard; there was a report of a double homicide on the 2600 block of Dorset Street.

A double homicide on Halloween night? *In Napa?* It sounded very much like John Carpenter's film *Halloween,* the one with the tag line "The Night He Came Home," about a mentally deranged man who begins stabbing young women left and right. Schectman could barely believe it. If the gossip he was hearing at the scene was true, this was a slasher movie come to life, the story of the year. It was all Schectman needed to hear; he jumped back into his car, drove to the station, and alerted the news desk. Soon all of Napa Valley would begin to know bits and pieces of what had happened on Dorset Street.

Inside the house, Detective Todd Shulman, a member of the investigative team who would ultimately become the lead detective on the case, climbed the stairs up to the second floor to witness the crime scene for himself. It was important, and he always tried to do that whenever possible, because, after all, photos can only show you so much—the size of the house, for instance. To say 2631 Dorset Street was small or compact doesn't begin to prepare you for how tiny, even doll-like, the house actually was. Barely 900 square feet, if that, the two-story house was worth more than half a million dollars, but only because it was in Napa. Anywhere else, the house might fetch $100,000 or even less. It was not without some charm, and it did have a big backyard, but it was very small. There were only fifteen stairs leading up the second-floor landing, which was slightly larger than a door laid flat on the ground. The bedroom facing the street, Adriane's bedroom, which was the scene of the carnage, measured only nine by twelve feet.

When Shulman stepped inside, he could see and smell blood everywhere. It's a smell you never forget. Traffic cops often can tell if a car crash is going to be nasty just by how much iron metallic smell is in the air; once you catch a whiff, you know it's bad. It was the same thing in this house. Shulman took in what he saw and muttered under his breath. He knew from other cops that this was no robbery; there seemed to be nothing of obvious value that was taken— nothing except, of course, two young lives.

"I was just struck by the violence of it," he said. "It was very evident from the blood that was there and the way the victims were positioned and the injuries they had sustained that you could tell that it was a very violent act that had occurred there."

Shulman's investigative mind took it all in. He had no autopsy to go on at this point, but he could use his own eyes and see that, whoever the murderer was, he had killed these women with a knife, and that meant one thing: this was a very personal crime. It was likely the killer knew at least one of his victims. How else to explain why he passed by the young lady on the first floor? Shulman knew there'd be endless hours of exhaustive work ahead of them, but on this first morning, he was more than willing to listen to what his gut was telling him.

"It just struck me that the person who did this must have been very physical," he said. "Must have been capable of overcoming two healthy, vibrant young girls and, you know, viciously attacking them and killing them in their own home.

"The blood evidence really speaks volumes

about what happened there. The little that I know about the blood patterns and things like that, you're able to start to get a picture in your mind of where these girls were and how they fought back those last moments of their lives."

Shulman was hoping against hope that the woman near the window—he didn't know yet that her name was Adriane Insogna—had wounded her attacker. She'd survived longer than her roommate, and from what he was hearing from the other cops, the surviving roommate had heard a violent struggle. With any luck, Adriane had scratched her attacker and made him bleed, which meant the cops would soon have his DNA and could begin comparing it to that of known offenders and anyone who'd had any contact with these young women. It could turn the whole case. Shulman hoped they'd be that lucky. And if the guy was wounded, well, he might even need a doctor's care. The detective turned to a nearby cop: "Let's make sure we alert every hospital here in the Valley and all the way to San Francisco to be on the lookout for anyone with suspicious injuries, knife wounds, scratches, anything like that."

Shulman directed other cops to make sure nothing was overlooked. Tracking dogs, bloodhounds, were unleashed to follow a scent, and they did pick one up, but it took them only to Highway 29 a few blocks away. Thanks to the highway, the murderer easily could have made a quick getaway, and he seemingly had. The entire block where the house sits on Dorset Street—a section that included about thirty homes—was sealed off. "Nobody enters, nobody leaves," was the operating principle. It was also important to walk Dorset Street thoroughly to make sure any evidence inadvertently dropped by the killer would be collected. Cops began to compile information on each neighbor to determine if anyone had a criminal record. Cars parked on the street were traced and searched. A canvass of the neighborhood did not turn up a single witness who had heard or seen anything.

Adriane's friend Christian Lee, who lived nearby and had been in her house, thinks he knows why no one heard anything. "Inside, they hold the noise fairly well. If you're next door, unless someone is screaming at the top of their lungs, it's going to be really difficult to hear people."

His analysis seems to ring true, because no one had called 911 except for Lauren Meanza. Shulman was frustrated, because he already knew from colleagues that Lauren, who was still nearby telling cops her story, had not actually seen the intruder. In fact, the traumatized roommate wasn't even sure the intruder was a man. The attacker nearly had run into her when he came down the stairs after killing the two other women, but at that point, Lauren had already turned to run out into the backyard. She could not provide anything in the way of eyewitness testimony. She'd heard a lot but had seen no one.

It was almost as though the killer were an apparition, a thought that led Shulman back to what everyone at the scene was buzzing about. Did this have anything to do with Halloween? Were the murders the work of a cult or a psycho who had seen one too many slasher movies? There was nothing to indicate the women had been killed in any ritualistic way, but Shulman could not ignore the obvious. Halloween was the elephant in the room; it was there whether he liked it or not, and he had to deal with it.

Shulman went outside to talk with Lauren again. He barely knew the victims' names at that point, and he knew he'd soon have to know every detail of their lives and whatever skeletons they had in their closets. Who liked them? Who didn't like them? Who were their boyfriends, girlfriends, mothers and fathers, families? Where were they from? Did they go to school? And the biggest question of all: Was one of them the target, and, if so, which one? He had a real whodunit on his hands, complicated by the presence of two victims and possibly two sets of motives.

The city of Napa had a small police department with only seventy-eight officers. They had investigated murders before, and they were not going to be on this one alone. Shulman knew he'd have plenty of help. In a case this high-profile, the higher-ups would want to form a major crimes task force with other detectives from other departments and the sheriff's office. It was likely they'd call on the FBI and the Justice Department for help with DNA analysis and profiling. What type of person would do something like this?

The only logical way to operate was to start with the inner circle of the young women and begin working out. That meant, first and foremost, boyfriends and ex-boyfriends.

The cops had a lead on a guy Adriane had spent a lot of time with in the past few days. What's more, they were told the relationship was rocky. Shulman looked at the name and took note of the address: Christian Lee lived nearby, much too close to ignore.

SIX

"She Was My Best Friend"

At 7:30 that morning, nine Napa police officers were knocking on the door of the house where Christian Lee lived with his brother and parents. Yes, his parents said, Christian lived there, and yes, he was home, sleeping soundly. After asking what this was all about, they were given a vague answer about a burglary in the neighborhood. "Just show us to his room," the cops said. A moment later, Christian, who was still sleeping, heard a loud knock on his door.

"I was startled, to say the least," he said when he opened the door and saw the cops. What was even creepier was the way they jumped back, as though *they* were afraid of *him*.

"Please come outside, sir," one of them said.

As he did, the nine cops, who weren't taking any chances, backed into the hall to keep their distance.

"Do you have any weapons or knives in your room?"

"I have a knife. Do you want me to get it for you?"

"No," said the cop in charge. "Just show us where it is, and we'll get it."

Christian pointed to a corner where he had a dusty old knife that he half forgot was even there. He hadn't picked it up in ages.

"What is this all about?"

"Do you have a friend named Adriane Insogna?" they asked, mispronouncing her name.

"Yes, why?" Christian began to get concerned. "Has something happened to her?"

"There was a burglary at her house, and there are some injuries. We'd like you to come down to the station house with us to answer some questions."

Christian agreed, pulled on some clothes, and soon found himself in a police cruiser. He gave them permission to search. "It was all so surreal," he said. "I didn't know what I was doing there or why, if there was a break-in at Adriane's house, they wanted to talk with me."

The female officer driving Christian to the police station refused to say anything more, just that they'd fill him in when he got there. Unbeknownst to Christian, the moment he set off for the station, the cops "tore apart" his room, he said later. "They took my clothes, my sheets, and dug up the backyard."

For fifteen minutes, Christian answered questions put to him by an unnamed detective. But the more the cop asked, the less Christian could concentrate. He wanted to know what was going on with his girlfriend. "Is she hurt? Did someone rape her?"

The cop was silent, but Christian couldn't stop asking questions: "You said there were injuries, but what kind of injuries? Can I talk to her? Can I see her?"

Again there was silence. Without any semblance of a satisfying answer, Christian began to cry. The cops left the room, but they were back in minutes. A decision had been made: since he wasn't giving them anything, maybe he needed to be confronted with the reality, whether he was responsible or not.

"Adriane is dead," one of them blurted out. "She was killed last night."

Christian could no longer hold it together.

He began to bawl as he never had before. The cops walked out, leaving him alone with his thoughts and emotions.

He and Adriane were not the perfect couple, although he considered her a "perfect person." Like Lauren, Christian had met Adriane at a volleyball class at Napa Community College. She'd smiled at him, and he was immediately drawn in, but so was his best friend, who wound up asking Adriane out first. "That pissed me off," he said later, but he made sure Adriane knew he was interested, too, and when it didn't work out with his best friend, Christian stepped in and asked her to go to a movie and dinner. They clicked, sort of, and began dating. But there were obvious problems. He admits to having a quick temper and a short fuse, something Adriane did not like and tried to help him with. And another small thing: she was a Giants fan, and he was a diehard Dodgers fan, enemies from birth.

They were both stubborn, they butted heads, and they argued with each other—a lot. In fact, it's one reason Lauren Meanza had given out his name to the cops so quickly. Whenever Christian visited the house on Dorset Street, he and Adriane seemed to get into a disagreement, and Lauren and Leslie heard it all. It became so bad and embarrassing that Christian began to resist going over there when he knew Adriane's roommates were home. He knew they thought ill of him. In fact, a lot of Adriane's girlfriends thought she deserved better than Christian was willing to offer and had let her know it. He was not one of their favorites.

But Adriane could not let Christian go. She knew he wouldn't commit to her because he'd been burned by a previous girlfriend, so she cut him some slack. But she also knew how to play him. She had joined what is called the 20–30 Club of Napa, a group of young professionals who get together for dinner and dancing. The club originated in Sacramento as a younger version of the Rotary Club, and, at least in the Napa branch, its members like to party. Their Web site is filled with photos of fun-filled dances. Some friends believe that Adriane joined so she'd have an alternative to waiting around for Christian to call. She'd go to the dances and even tell Christian about the interesting men she met. In fact, she had told Christian about a new guy she'd given her number to just the week before at the group's annual Halloween party.

So the relationship with Christian was full of game playing, and there were signs that Adriane felt she should not keep it going. She had complained so often about Christian that her girlfriends had soured on them as a couple and told Adriane she could do better. Because of that, Adriane wouldn't tell her friends when she and Christian reignited their on-again, off-again relationship, as they had just a day before she was murdered. It was just too embarrassing.

The day before Halloween, Saturday, October 30, Christian had worked late at his bartending job at Downtown Joe's. Adriane had told him to call her when he got off from work, but he didn't get off until 4:00 a.m., the very early hours of Halloween. "I figured it was late," he said. "And so I went and partied with my friends across the street from work. And she had sent me a text message saying that she missed me and she wanted to see me that night, and to come home. I didn't even have to think about it. I just drove home right away. She came over to my house. And we just cuddled, and we talked all night. And we watched TV. I don't think we fell asleep until about six or seven in the morning."

The last time Christian saw Adriane was when she came back to his house on Halloween night at about 9:30 p.m. and stayed for an hour. The last he heard from Adriane was the text message in which she told him she wished every day could be like the one they'd just had. Both of them soon fell asleep at their respective houses, and that's all Christian knew until the cops woke him up.

He told the cops all of that when they finally returned to the interrogation room. "They checked through my cell phone for when she called and checked text messages she sent me," he said.

They seemed to believe his story, but they were not taking any chances and took vials of his blood. He understood—he was her boyfriend, after all, and he knew they had to verify his story. They asked if he could think of anyone who would want to harm Adriane. He thought of two people, but it seemed ridiculous. One of them was a past girlfriend of his. He didn't think she was really capable of harming anyone that way, but "she hated Adriane." The other person Christian thought of was the guy Adriane said she'd met at a Halloween party the weekend before. Those were the only two people who might have a motive for harming Adriane, but even Christian couldn't believe it. He didn't think he knew anyone who would want to kill someone.

After three hours, the cops released him. He was alone, thinking of how he'd planned to ask Adriane to move in with him, how he'd planned for them to get their own place. Now she'd never know any of that. "She was my best friend; I could tell her anything," he thought. He consoled himself with the thought that, at least at the end, their relationship had been going well. He cried all the way home and all the next day. He thought he had been cleared, but the next day, he drove by Dorset Street just to see what was going on. "By the time I hit the end of that street and made my turn, I noticed there was a cop car behind me," he said. "And then I went farther down, and I switched lanes. And he kept stayin' behind me. And then I went over the overpass and he wasn't there any longer. And then next thing I knew, there was another truck behind me that was following me whenever I switched lanes. Don't know for sure if I was being followed, but it felt like it."

It was still much too early in the Adriane Insogna and Leslie Mazzara murder investigation to rule anyone out. The reverberations of that four-minute rampage—that selfish, insane act that killed two vibrant young women—were just starting to be felt across the country and even halfway around the world.

SEVEN

A Strong Woman

While it was still Monday, November 1, in the United States, down in Australia—some nineteen hours ahead—it was already Tuesday, and a glorious day in Sydney was in full swing. The sunshine was peeking in and out of the clouds, the air was cool, and the three American friends felt especially good. It was the fourth day of a seventeen-day holiday in the Land Down Under, but it was the best one yet. Arlene Allen and friends Lauren and Rita from the Napa Valley had spent the morning climbing the fabled Sydney Harbor Bridge.

Making that climb on the bridge—nicknamed the "the coathanger" by locals—to take in the sights over the beautiful Sydney Harbor has become a "must do" for any American visiting Australia. It's a fairly strenuous climb; it takes three and a half hours to get to the top, and it's not for the fainthearted, seeing as how the bridge rises 440 feet above the harbor. The friends, all women of a certain age, had donned jumpsuits supplied by the climbing company and had themselves attached to the railings, designed to prevent accidents. "There is nothing that you have that is not attached to you," Arlene Allen said. "Even your hat has a little string on it." It took them a while, but they completed the climb and were proud of themselves for having the gumption to get all the way to the top.

"It was a really incredible experience," said Allen. "As I climbed up there, I just had this wonderful feeling, almost kind of like euphoria, and when I got to the top, that feeling was just so overwhelming. I felt as free as a bird."

Allen's youngest daughter, Allison, lived in Melbourne, and so Arlene was the instigator for the trip. A twice-divorced mother from Texas now living in Calistoga, California, Arlene had two other daughters who lived near her in California: Lexi, her oldest, and Adriane, her middle child, who was living in Napa. Arlene was closest to Adriane because of geography and circumstances. Adriane was everything she could want in a daughter; the two had a loving relationship, and Adriane often included her mother in her activities, more as a friend than as a mother. Just that past summer, Adriane had invited Arlene to a San Francisco Giants baseball game and later to watch the July 4 fireworks from her rooftop on Dorset Street. Adriane had her usual close group of friends there, but she knew Arlene would fit in just fine.

Arlene understood Adriane's likes and dislikes, and she had experienced a moment on top of the bridge that she just knew Adriane, an engineer, would love. "She's always been fascinated by bridges, and when she was young, she pressed her nose up against the car window, and every time we'd pass a bridge, she'd ask me, 'How can that bridge go over so much water?'"

So when Arlene stood atop the Harbor Bridge and looked down onto another engineering marvel, the Sydney Opera House, she could only imagine what Adriane would think. "I was thinking, 'Wow, I can't wait for Adriane to see this. She will really love this.'"

Arlene had no idea that her beloved daughter Adriane was dead. A horrible twist of fate placed Adriane where she should not have been at the moment she was murdered. Adriane was supposed to be in Hawaii on October 31; in fact, she had been very much looking forward to it. Her good friend Lily Prudhomme, who worked with Adriane in the Napa Sanitation District, had been scheduled to get married in Hawaii that Halloween weekend and had invited Adriane to the ceremony. But then, over the previous summer, Lily had broken up with her fiancé, Eric Copple, and the wedding had been canceled. After losing out on her Hawaii wedding, Lily had instead agreed to go to Australia with Adriane, and the two friends were scheduled to make the trip in mid-November, just two weeks after Adriane's mother returned to California. Lily and Eric were now back together, but the wedding had been put off to some future date.

As Arlene looked at the Sydney Opera House and thought how much her daughter would love the view, it was already too late. This was a view Adriane would never experience.

After climbing down from the bridge, Arlene, Lauren, and Rita went to a local pub for lunch and discovered a big crowd. It was the day of the Melbourne Cup, a horse race not unlike the Kentucky Derby. The Australians, gregarious and known for their hospitality, were having a wonderful time in the pub and invited the women to place a small wager on which horse would win the race. "It was a really fun, joyful day," Arlene said.

As the women walked back to their hotel, Rita split off to search for a Laundromat. "We arrived back at our hotel room about a quarter till five in the afternoon to change clothes to go out for dinner," Arlene said.

Arlene stepped into her room and stopped. There was a piece of paper on the floor. She picked it up and saw that there were a couple of messages there. One was to call her daughter Lexi, the other to call her daughter Allison. "Oh, no," she instinctively thought, "something's wrong." It was one thing for Allison to call; after all, they were supposed to rendezvous later that week. But why would Lexi call?

Arlene's first thought was that perhaps something had happened to her own mother, who was quite old and frail.

"Oh, God," Arlene said to Lauren. "There's probably something wrong with my mother."

"Well, call her and find out," Lauren said.

Faced with the choice of calling Lexi in California, where it was now 10:00 p.m. on Monday night, or calling Allison, who was in the same time zone, Arlene made the easy choice and called Allison, her youngest.

Allison picked up the phone immediately. "Hi, honey," Arlene said nonchalantly. "I got your message. What's up?"

Allison got right to the point: "Mom, an intruder broke into Adriane's house, and Adriane and Leslie are dead."

Arlene, a strong woman who had handled everything life had thrown at her up to that point—two broken marriages and the responsibility of raising three young girls on not much money—could not comprehend this. What was Allison telling her? It made no sense, no sense at all.

"Adriane's dead?" Arlene asked.

At that point, Lauren, who was in the same room, crossed the room to Arlene and looked into her friend's eyes. Lauren wasn't sure she'd heard Arlene correctly. "I was thinking, 'She said *who* was dead?' "

"Yes," Allison said into the phone. "She's dead."

Arlene still couldn't or wouldn't believe it. "She's dead?" she asked again.

"Mom, Adriane's dead," Allison responded.

Allison, who had heard the news from her sister much earlier in the day, had been working on getting them on a flight that would take the two of them back to California immediately.

She tried to tell her mother that she'd be there soon and to give her the flight information for their trip the next day. But Arlene would not hear another word. She collapsed on the bed, and Lauren grabbed the phone. Allison began telling Lauren about her travel arrangements, but at the point, Lauren couldn't absorb much information, either.

"When are you going to be here?" Lauren asked.

"My plane gets in at 10:00, and I should be at your hotel by 11:00."

"Okay," Lauren said. "We'll wait up for you, and I'll make sure I'm at the door. I'll make sure I'm there to open the door for you."

Lauren hung up, and the two women hugged each other, sobbing.

Arlene was wailing, "She's dead! My daughter's dead!"

Moments later—it seemed like just a second, really—the phone rang again. It was Arlene's oldest daughter, Lexi, calling from the United States.

"Mom, it's Lexi."

"Lexi, I can't," Arlene said. "I know, I just found out, and I can't talk to you right now."

She hung up and went back to crying while Lauren tried to comfort her.

"We didn't know anything at that point," Lauren said later. "Just that someone broke in and killed these two women. After we settled down, we started thinking, 'What could have happened? What happened? How did it happen? Who did it?' "

It was then that Rita returned to the room, and she couldn't figure out what had happened. Why was everyone crying? Both women told her the news, and she slumped onto her bed, unable to absorb what was happening half a world away. After consoling Arlene as best they could under the circumstances, Lauren and Rita left her to gather her thoughts. When they returned a short time later, Arlene told her friends she had made a decision: "You've got to finish the trip for me."

Lauren had mixed feelings, but eventually she decided that her friend would need her a lot more in a couple of weeks when things had settled down. When Arlene returned to the States, she would have her daughters and many friends and supporters around, at least for a short time. Lauren decided then and there that she would be Arlene's support system for the long term. She would stand by her friend when everyone else returned to their lives and Arlene was left alone. In the meantime, Lauren wondered what she could do at that moment to console her close friend.

Then something struck her. It was a question no mother wants to hear, but Lauren thought it necessary to raise it. "Arlene, where is Adriane going to be buried?"

"I don't know," Arlene said. "I can't even think about that."

"Well," said Lauren, trying to get her friend to focus on something, anything, "it's something you need to think about—unfortunately."

Lauren had a thought. Her father-in-law was buried in Sonoma in a cemetery called Evergreen in Knight's Valley. Arlene had visited the cemetery a number of times with Lauren, and Lauren knew that her friend loved it because it was rustic and peaceful. But it was a restricted cemetery, and you had to be a ten-year resident of the area to be buried there.

"Listen," Lauren said, "I know you don't want to think about this now, but wherever Adriane is buried, you're going to want to be nearby, and I think she's eligible to be buried there because you lived in Knight's Valley for a long time. Think about it; it's just a piece of information for you to take back with you."

"How am I ever going to get through this, Lauren?"

"Just the way you always have," Lauren said. "You're a very strong woman, and you'll get through this."

Lauren took her friend in her arms and rocked her gently.

EIGHT

"Tell Us Everything"

The next day, Arlene and Allison boarded a plane to make the twelve-hour trip back to San Francisco for what was the worst flight of their lives. They'd had no sleep and now had to be locked in an airplane when all they wanted was to get back to Napa and ask as many questions as possible. They cried separately and together but tried their best to shield their unbearable grief from the other passengers. There were just too many questions, and they had no answers. The world had stopped making sense.

"It was just so hard," Arlene said. "Allison had a difficult time during the flight. She disappeared for a while. I went to find her, and she came out of the restroom area, and she was just devastated. It was clear she was sobbing, and it just broke my heart. Honestly.

"But I think that it was a real blessing that I was there, to be with Allison. So she didn't have to make that plane trip alone."

Just seven months before, Adriane had accompanied her sister to Melbourne to help her set up her new life with a new job for Oakley sunglasses. "It wasn't a vacation for Adriane," Arlene says. "She wanted to help Allison get a car and make sure she was doing okay and not all by herself. That was how she was."

Slumping into her airline seat, Arlene closed her eyes and remembered the last time she had seen Adriane. The doting daughter—the one who had always been closest to her mother—had driven Arlene, Lauren, and Rita to the airport, and the women had stopped on the way for something to eat at In-N-Out Burger. Adriane was very excited for them and more than a little interested, because she and Lily would be taking the same trip in a matter of weeks. This time, Adriane would be going on vacation. There were many questions and jokes flying back and forth, and before Arlene and her friends went through airport security, Adriane gave them big hugs. "It was a very, very happy parting," Arlene rememberd. Adriane was supposed to pick them up upon their return. "See you when you get back," she'd said.

Thoughts like that made it impossible for Arlene to sleep on the flight, and by the time she and Allison arrived in Napa, Arlene had been awake for more than forty hours. She thought bitterly about how she'd been treated for depression *before* hearing her lovely daughter was dead. What chance did she have that any treatment would work now? But she knew she needed something and had called ahead to let her doctor know what had happened. He insisted she stop at his office before even going home. "I wanted to see if I could maybe get some sleep aids or something to help deal with this," Arlene said.

The moment Arlene and Allison walked into the office, it was like the seas parting. They were ushered in immediately to see the doctor, who had known Arlene for years. He was with a patient, but no patient was going through what Arlene was going through at that moment. The doctor even had arranged for a grief counselor to be there to speak with Arlene and help her through the unimaginable.

"He gave me some good pointers on how to deal with what was coming up, and we came home and immediately went down to Napa to meet with the police," she said.

* * *

It was Wednesday night. The police had many questions, but in some ways, it all boiled down to one. They wanted to know everything. Did Adriane have any enemies? Did they know of anyone who might want to harm her? Had she mentioned anyone strange recently?

Arlene could barely help them. She had heard from Adriane about some nasty crank calls she'd received the year before, but that was in a different house. Other than that, she drew a blank.

"That's what's so strange about this case," Arlene said. "Because I couldn't think of any reason someone might want Adriane dead. I couldn't think of a single reason. The only possibility I could bring to mind was that it might have had something to do with Leslie, because she was meeting so many new people. And she might have crossed paths with someone who wasn't quite right. Adriane was surrounded by people she had known for years, a long time. This is just something I believed in my heart. I believed that Leslie had been the target and that Adriane had come to her aid because that is very much Adriane's personality."

Leslie's family and friends, meanwhile, were just as shocked as Adriane's family.

NINE

The Godfather

The wineries in the Napa Valley are known the world over for their elegant beauty and their representation of the good life, but no estate has more Old World charm than the stately chateau at the Niebaum-Coppola winery in Rutherford, just a ten-minute drive north of Napa on Highway 29. The winery changed its name to Rubicon in March 2006 because "Mr. Coppola wanted to put the focus solely on the wine." The main estate house was built in the nineteenth century by a former Finnish sea captain named Gustave Niebaum, and it was restored to its full glory in the twentieth century by acclaimed film director Francis Ford Coppola, who made the fabled *Godfather* movies. Soon after conquering Hollywood, Coppola began searching for a family estate away from San Francisco; it didn't take long to discover Napa just forty-five minutes away, and in 1975, he purchased 1,500 acres of the Niebaum estate and moved his family there. In 1995, the profits from the film *Bram Stoker's Dracula* allowed him to buy the entire property. Since then, he has created memorable wines and built a full film studio on the premises. The second floor of the estate house has become the unofficial Coppola museum, with his Oscars on prominent display. Because of the Coppola mystique, the winery, more than most others, is an exciting place, and the beautiful grounds, with their fountains and ivy-covered house, are immensely popular with tourists.

But something ugly brought the winery workers together on the morning of November 1, 2004. The head of human resources called an unusual meeting for everyone on-site, and in minutes, the area around the main tasting room was filled with dozens of workers curious to know what was going on. Coppola himself was away that day. "This is," the manager told the group, "by far the worst thing I've ever had to do. It is my sad duty to report that our Leslie, Leslie Mazzara, is dead."

A collective gasp filled the room. No one could believe what they were hearing, and before anyone asked the question, the human resources woman went on to say, "Leslie was murdered along with her roommate last night by someone who broke into their house. We really don't know anything else."

Leslie had worked at the winery for only six months, but already she'd made her mark. She had been promoted twice, and everyone knew who she was. Like any winery, Niebaum-Coppola has separate fiefdoms—the vintners, the pourers, the tour guides, even the maintenance staff—and each group pretty much sticks to its own. Leslie was an exception, able to move freely within each social group and comfortable in them all. She also had a close circle of girlfriends she'd met there, women her own age with whom she'd go out to restaurants and bars several nights a week.

It was the first and only place Leslie had applied for a job when she first landed in Napa. According to friends, she just walked in and said, "Hi, I'm Leslie, are y'all hiring?" and they were, at least for someone with her looks and charm. She got $11.50 an hour to start, and her first job there was meeting and greeting the tourists at the concierge desk when they first walked in. One can only imagine how they reacted to someone with such a pronounced Southern accent working up in Napa. Somehow it worked, and she clicked at the winery. Leslie had even met the famous Mr. Coppola a few times. She joked that she hoped he'd discover her, and close friends knew she was only half joking. After all, she always had high aspirations.

Leslie often joked about it with her close friend Kelly McCorkle, saying, "Mr. Coppola hasn't quite discovered me yet, but he's going to one day." They would laugh about it. "She really enjoyed working for that winery," McCorkle said.

Coppola is no absentee owner. He lives on part of the estate and is very hands-on. It's not unusual for tourists to find him sitting outside or in a café reading a book, and he's signed more than his share of wine bottles brought to him by film fans and wine enthusiasts alike. The Thursday before Leslie's death, the winery had sponsored one of its Cavern Club dances. Held every other week during good weather, the dances are a bonding experience for the estate's workers and locals who bring families and friends and cut loose. Coppola, reportedly a good dancer and a salsa fan, had been at the dance that night, a few days before the murder.

Leslie loved to dance, and at the club, she was in her natural surroundings.

And now the workers were confronted with the news that this larger-than-life presence was dead; it was a devastating blow. "No one knew what to do," said one woman who was there. "Everyone was just hugging each other and crying. It was unbelievable that someone with a personality like Leslie's was not going to be there any longer."

TEN

The Beauty Queen

While the police were able to identify Leslie Mazzara quickly as an employee of the Niebaum-Coppola winery, they were having less success with tracking down her family. There was a lot of confusion in those first hours of the investigation, and Leslie, unlike Adriane, was not local. Word of the killings spread rapidly in the Napa Valley, and soon everyone who knew Adriane—even her mother and sister in Australia—had heard the horrible news. It was not that way with Leslie's family and friends; they heard in dribs and drabs.

Part of the problem for the police was that Leslie was from Anderson, South Carolina, but the Napa police were not immediately sure of the location of her next of kin. Complicating the matter was that Leslie's mother—Cathy Harrington—and Leslie's older brothers—Paul and Andy Clem—had different last names from Leslie and from each other, and they lived in different parts of the country. The police did not want to inform the wrong family and put them through hell, so, before making a mistake, they began putting out feelers across the United States that eventually drifted back to the right people in Leslie's hometown.

Renee Tollison, a court reporter from South Carolina, was one of the first to hear. Tollison is a co-director of the Miss Williamston beauty pageant, an event that Leslie Mazzara won in 2002. The contest was something of a lark for Leslie, who later graduated with a philosophy degree from the University of Georgia, home of her beloved Bulldogs football team. One of Leslie's best friends, Kelly McCorkle, was more the beauty contest type, and, in fact, Kelly was Miss South Carolina in 2002. Tall, lithe, and a stunning brunette beauty with a body to match, Kelly has entered multiple beauty contests and won her share. Leslie was different. She was attractive but did not have classic good looks like

Kelly's. Leslie was petite, not tall. The Miss Williamston contest and the subsequent Miss South Carolina contest were the only beauty pageants Leslie ever entered.

Kelly and Leslie met the summer after ninth grade when both were studying at the Greenville Ballet.

"I walked up to her and said, 'Hi, I'm Kelly McCorkle.'"

"Oh, I know who you are," Kelly remembered Leslie saying in her own impish way. "I sat beside you all summer."

Kelly was taken aback. "What?"

"Yeah, don't you remember?" she said, cracking up. Leslie explained that she had sat in a summer class next to a chair that had Kelly's name tag on it.

"My plans had changed, and I couldn't make it," Kelly said.

"Well, I sure know your name," Leslie countered. "I guess it's just destiny that we were meant to be side by side."

"She was right, because we've been side by side ever since," Kelly said.

Kelly had begun entering beauty contests for the scholarship money that helped put her through college. She eventually competed in three Miss South Carolina contests, winning once. Leslie was curious about the crowns. She would try one on every time she went to Kelly's house.

"Can I have one of your crowns?" she finally asked.

"No, you go get your own."

"Do you think I could?"

"Leslie, I have no doubt."

With Kelly's help, Leslie entered the Miss Williamston contest. Renee Tollison, who was in her first year of running the pageant, got to know Leslie well. It was a learning experience for both of them, but the women bonded in more ways than that. "Leslie's mother was out in California, and so we sort of filled a need for her. She called us her surrogate mommies," she said, referring to herself and co-director Danette Hanks. Leslie's talent was dancing; she had studied classical ballet for fifteen years.

"Leslie was just a beautiful spirit inside and out. Her sparkling green eyes lit up the room when she smiled. She was a beautiful dancer. We were real happy when she won."

But winning was only the beginning for Leslie. She was determined that her reign as Miss Williamston mean something—and she really meant it. She had been searching for a platform she believed in, and Tollison inadvertently found it for her thanks to her job as a court reporter. Just before meeting Leslie, Tollison had been deeply affected by a trial she had been assigned to: the beating death of a four-year-old girl named Stephanie Carter. Stephanie's life was short in time but long in horror. Family members had tortured the little girl in the most horrible ways imaginable. "Part of what happened with this little girl," Tollison said, "is that she was locked inside a tiny bathroom for weeks at a time."

When Leslie heard Tollison talk about Stephanie, she decided her platform would be child abuse prevention. She worked with legislators to help pass a bill that became Stephanie's Law, requiring reports of suspected child abuse to be recorded to help officials detect patterns of abuse. But that wasn't enough for Leslie. When she learned that a memorial fund had been set up to build a cottage for abused children in Stephanie's name at the Calvary Home for Children in Anderson, Leslie decided she was going to raise money for that home. "Leslie was very passionate," Tollison said. "She had a deep place in her soul for children who were hurting."

The women brainstormed around Tollison's kitchen table for hours, thinking of how they could hammer their message home, and Leslie came up with an idea. She decided to go to the

Anderson mall, pick a spot where a lot of people walked by, and tape off a small area that was the exact size of the bathroom that Stephanie was forced to live in. It would be a Sit-athon. Leslie put a chair in the tiny spot and sat there hour after hour, talking to people about Stephanie's short life and what she was doing and getting them to contribute money to build the cottage in the little girl's honor. Leslie called it the "Sit for Stephanie." She raised $982 that day, and a later Sit-athon at a farmer's market raised $937.

Looking back, Tollison shook her head at Leslie's own story. "It's just tragic to think that someone so passionate about this ugliness in our society would now become a victim at someone else's hands."

At 8:15 p.m. on Monday, November 1, 2004, Renee Tollison had no idea of the tragedy that had unfolded thousands of miles away. She remembers that "about 8:30, I got a call from my best friend, my co-director, Danette Hanks."

"Have you heard from Leslie recently?"

"No, not lately, not since she judged our last pageant back in March. A few e-mails back and forth is all. Why?"

Hanks hesitated. Her news was so bad she

didn't know if she could even say it. "Oh, Renee, Rick [her husband] just got a call from a reporter out in California. There's a Leslie Mazzara out there who's been killed. They weren't sure if it was the same girl, so they asked Rick to e-mail some pictures, and then they called back and said it was definitely Leslie."

Tollison couldn't help but cry all over again as she recalled the story. "Danette explained that the reporter said the story was going to break all over the news, and they knew she had family here and wanted us to know.

"We didn't know the phone number [of Leslie's family], but Danette and I both knew where they lived. We couldn't imagine them hearing this on the news, so we went over there to tell them or at least to be there for some comfort if they already knew."

The women went first to the house owned by Leslie's brother Paul (known as PJ) Clem, but he wasn't home, so they rushed to Leslie's grandmother's house. Anyone who knew Leslie knew Grammy. Leslie talked about her incessantly, so much so that Judy Harrington liked to joke that most people thought her real name was Grammy. She was a strong presence in Leslie's life and a strong woman besides. "She didn't know, so we broke the news to her," Tollison said. "She got Paul on the phone, and Paul came over, and we were just all in shock."

"When I heard that Leslie had been murdered, I thought maybe it was a drive-by shooting or something," Paul said. "But the more we became aware of it, the harder it was to take. The idea that someone had broken into the house and done this in the night . . . the first thought in my mind was serial killer. It was Halloween, Halloween night, so I thought serial killer."

Paul called his brother, Andy, who was at the airport and about to go on his honeymoon to Spain. He said he immediately thought his sister had been killed by some deranged serial killer. "Being from the East Coast, you think out in California it's a different world," he said.

Andy kept repeating one thing to his brother over and over: "This can't be true. This can't be true."

Andy wanted to stay, but he and his bride were about to get on the plane. The timing was horrible. In the end, he decided to go ahead with the honeymoon. While Paul and Grammy and Tollison and Hanks sat around trying to figure out what was going on, there was a knock on the door.

It was a heartbroken Kelly McCorkle, who had just heard the news.

For most of 2004, Leslie's close friend had been living in Washington, D.C., working for then-Congressman Jim DeMint. It was a campaign year, which meant it was a crazy time for any politician, and the days around Halloween were the busiest because there were only a few days left before Election Day. Kelly had gone home to Greenville, South Carolina, to help the congressman get the votes out and was sitting in her car in a parking lot that Monday evening when her mother called.

"Kelly, you need to get home. You need to get home right now."

Kelly was hit with a sinking feeling; the tone of her mother's voice was urgent and extremely serious. "Mom, just tell me. Tell me what it is. Just tell me what it is right now."

"You need to come home. You just need to come home."

"No, Mom, I'm not going to be driving panicked because there's something wrong and I don't know what it is. Just tell me now."

"Well, Kelly, we just got a phone call, and we think something happened to Leslie."

"Leslie?"

"Kelly, they think she was murdered. We need your help to try to identify that it's her out in California. The police are having a hard time figuring out if it was Leslie Mazzara from Anderson, South Carolina, and they need to know if she worked at a winery."

"Yes, yes, Leslie does work at a winery. Oh, my God! I can't believe it!"

Crying hysterically, Kelly raced home to find out more, thinking it was impossible. "Honestly, I didn't believe it was her. I thought, 'This is not right.' "

When she arrived home, her father looked up the news on the Internet, and then Kelly drove over to where Leslie's family was holed up. "I just pretty much ran to Leslie's family and just talked to them all night, waiting for information and trying to get answers and just comfort them a little. They knew how close Leslie and I were, and I just wanted to be with them. It was just waiting and waiting and waiting. There were no answers."

Paul suddenly remembered Leslie's other close friend, Amy Brown. "I gotta call Amy," he told Kelly.

"You go ahead," she said.

As Paul dialed Amy, Kelly just sat there, pressing Leslie's number on the speed dial of her cell phone. "I must have called it at least twenty-five times, and she never answered," she said crying. "She never answered."

ELEVEN

"Talk to You Later"

Amy Brown was fifteen when she met Leslie. The girls had gone to their local church in Anderson and were headed to a local pizza joint with all the other teens. But when they walked out to the parking lot late one day, everyone they knew was gone. Amy and Leslie went to different high schools, and though they knew each other by sight, they had never really talked.

"So Leslie turned around and said, 'Well, I guess we're gonna ride together,' " Amy said.

Leslie had a permit and a car, so off they went. It was the beginning of a beautiful friendship. The girls became something more than sisters, not surprising given Amy's firecracker personality. She was every bit as spunky as Leslie was. The two developed an inseparable bond. "I actually don't remember not being with Leslie," Amy said. "I think our friendship is more than a friendship. It's a little bit closer. It's even a little bit closer than sisters. We were just inseparable after that day in the parking lot. Leslie was my soul mate."

The girls had sleepovers every weekend, mostly at Amy's home. Throughout her life, Leslie told friends that she yearned for a more traditional family life and found it over at Amy's (as well as Kelly's). Amy played basketball and softball, while Leslie skated and danced ballet, but they supported each other every inch of the way. "I went to her recitals, and she never missed a game of mine. And we hung out all the time."

Not surprisingly, Leslie was the maid of honor at Amy's wedding in late September 2004. By that time, Leslie was already in Napa, and when she came east, she stayed over at Amy's house just like old times. But there was something different about this trip—an offhanded comment that Leslie made that, in retrospect, seemed to be a foreshadowing of what was to come. Amy vividly remembered what Leslie said as they were hauling her luggage up the stairs, her very nice luggage.

"Where'd ya get these bags?"

"Oh, from an ex-boyfriend," Leslie said.

Amy nodded. She knew Leslie's way with men. The ones who had money thought they could buy her with expensive gifts. One had given her a car, one took her on a cruise but Leslie ultimately made up her own mind, and both of those guys were now ex-boyfriends.

"They're heavy," Amy said about the luggage. "Must've been expensive."

"Well, you know me, Amy. I'm just a brat. I get all these things, and I just know that I'm gonna get mine in the end."

That was a weird comment from out of left field, even for Leslie, Amy recalled. "That made me very uneasy. I'm sure she knew nothing of what she was saying. It was just a comment about how people were always buying her things and she never asked for anything, but she's pampered and she's beautiful, and I just got a strange feeling that day."

Except for that, everything between the friends was normal. The wedding went off smoothly, and Leslie flew back to her new life in Napa.

The day after Halloween, Amy heard the phone ringing in her house, but she was taking a nap and let the answering machine pick it up. She got up and leisurely hit "Play."

"Hey, it's PJ. I got some . . . I gotta tell you something. Call me back."

From his tone, Amy knew that whatever it was, it wasn't good. She suspected something had happened to Grammy. "And then I thought, 'No, if something happened to Grammy, Leslie would call me.' "

PJ almost never called Amy unless Leslie was around, so she called him back right away. "I've got some bad news," he said. "Are you alone?"

"What? What is it? You've gotta tell me."

"Well, Leslie's been killed."

Like everyone else who heard the news, Amy thought it was impossible, some bizarre case of mistaken identity. Her questions to PJ seem silly now, but it was a coping mechanism, a way to avoid reality.

"Are you sure? Are you positive?"

"Yes."

Amy sank to the floor, slamming down hard. PJ might as well have told her the world had stopped revolving; that's what it felt like. Her glasses fell off her face. Nothing was making sense. "How? You gotta tell me how. What happened? Are you sure? Are you sure it was Leslie? Was it a car wreck?"

"I can't even say this, Amy. But Leslie was murdered last night. She was stabbed to death."

Amy refused to accept it. "This isn't real. This

can't be happening. This has to be a mistake. It has to be."

"Where's Thad?" PJ said, asking about Amy's newlywed husband.

"He's at work."

"Well, you gotta hang up, and you need to get him home right now."

She called her husband, told him the news, and hung up the phone. "There was a knock on my door, and it was my aunt. Suddenly, people were surrounding me. Everyone was there to comfort me just as quickly as I got the phone call. It was just kind of an out-of-body experience. You just have so many things going through your head, and you can't accept any of it."

She collapsed in their arms and allowed everyone to care for her. As the night wore on, Amy began to think about the last time she had spoken to Leslie. It was just the day before, on Halloween; the close friends had had three phone conversations that day. "We talked about nothing, what she was gonna do that day. Even if we had nothing to really say," Amy said, "we'd talk for an hour. That day was no different."

Their last conversations were typically nothing serious. "We talked about nothing a lot, and when I got off the phone, my husband would say, 'What did y'all talk about?' and I'd say,

'Nothing' and he'd say, 'How do you talk about nothing for two hours?' "

In the afternoon, Leslie had called Amy on her cell phone while she was driving home, following her husband's car.

"Whatcha doin'?" Leslie asked.

Amy eyed a train crossing she was trying to get to before the train came by.

"I'm trying to beat this train," she said.

Just then, a convertible cut her off. "Darn, this car just cut me off. I don't think I'm gonna make it."

"You go, girl. Beat him."

"Yeah, you're right. I am gonna beat this train."

Amy raced to the next crossing, but she was too late. The train came by, and the crossings came down.

"Keep going, girl, you can beat it."

"Nah, I think I'm just gonna sit here and talk to you."

They talked for a while until Amy asked her, "Whatcha doin' for Halloween?"

"I was gonna go to a party," Leslie said, "but the girls and I discussed handing out candy in the neighborhood, so that's what I'm gonna do. I just want a relaxing night."

"Okay, I'll talk to you later. Love you."

"I love you, too," Leslie said for the last time.

TWELVE

God Help Her

While word of Leslie's death now was spreading quickly in South Carolina, Leslie's own mother had not heard a thing. Cathy Harrington was a newly ordained Unitarian minister living in Ludington, Michigan, a cute little tourist town right on Lake Michigan. Ludington is a place where a lot of Chicagoans have second homes—a choice location. Reverend Harrington was a minister at the People's Church. She'd only had the job for a few short months at that point and was still getting to know her new congregants, and they her.

At around 8:00 p.m., she answered her cell phone while driving back from dinner at a friend's house. It was her sister Susan calling from

California, and she sounded excited and worried.

"Have you heard from Leslie today?" Susan asked.

"Not today," Cathy said. "I spoke to her yesterday, though. Why?"

"I don't know. Would you call her and see if you can get hold of her?"

"Why, Susan, what's going on?"

"Well, I don't know, but Nina [Susan's best friend] just called me and said her landlady heard something on the news. This is all secondhand information, but the landlady told my friend she'd heard on the news something about two girls getting murdered in Napa."

Only months before, Cathy had been the one to persuade her daughter Leslie to move to Napa after she'd mentioned that she was struggling with every twenty-something's angst: what to do with her life. Leslie was thinking about graduate school or possibly a career in law. Cathy, who became serious about her religious vocation later in life, was finishing up her religious schooling in Berkeley. She told her daughter to stop worrying about graduate school and have some fun. "Why don't you come out here and pour some wine until you get your head together?" she'd said.

Leslie had always wanted to get closer to her

mom and never hesitated when her mother invited her, no matter how far she had to travel. When she was in college, she followed her mother to Alaska three summers in a row, just to be close to her, both physically and emotionally. It was a recurring dilemma for Leslie, a need to be closer to her mother, who, after Leslie turned eighteen, was usually off on an adventure of her own.

As Cathy listened to her sister's secondhand gossip about the Napa murders, she grew angry. "Susan, why would you think that was Leslie? Why are you calling me?"

Susan hesitated. "I don't know. Look, just call her cell phone, okay? And call me back when you talk to her, okay?"

Cathy immediately punched in her daughter's number and left a message. Minutes later, when she pulled her car into her driveway, she spotted a police car near her house and had a sinking feeling. Could the gossip possibly be true? But then the police car pulled away. "Guess it's just a stray dog or something," Cathy thought, feeling suddenly relieved.

The instant she went into her home, the phone rang again. It was Susan. "Did you get hold of Leslie?"

"No. What's going on? Why would you think this?"

"Because they said on the news that the house was on Dorset Street in Napa."

Cathy felt as if she might faint, but she calmed herself down and knew what she had to do. She asked the operator for the phone number of the Napa police department. "My name is Cathy Harrington, and my daughter lives in Napa and I'm trying to find out if she's okay," Cathy told the dispatcher.

"What's your daughter's name, ma'am?"

"Leslie Mazzara."

"We've been waiting for you to call. Give me your number; I'll have a detective call you right back."

When nobody called back right away, Cathy hoped for the best. "I knew that one girl survived, so for about an hour, I was praying it was Leslie," she said.

But she couldn't wait all night. Cathy redialed the police, and she was patched through to a detective. He asked if the Ludington police had been out to her house and seemed upset when she said no. Napa Police Commander Jeff Troendly later said that the Ludington police had been assigned the task of notifying Cathy, but apparently, signals were crossed.

"Ma'am, your daughter was killed along with another young lady in the house. I'm very sorry."

A grief counselor came on the line to talk to Cathy, but she barely heard what was said. This time, Cathy knew what she had to do—she had to go west and be near her daughter. The rest of the night was a blur. Cathy found a close friend to fly with, got on the Internet, and bought tickets for the following day. "Thank God, he was able to take off work and fly with me so I wouldn't have to fly across the country alone," she said. "It was very bizarre to have to fly having just heard the news that your daughter had been murdered."

The final indignity occurred at the security check-in at the airport. Because Cathy had purchased her ticket so close in time to when she was flying, she was deemed a security risk and was pulled out of line for a complete body search. "I had to be frisked, and it felt like such a physical violation," she said. "With all that was going on, it was just a nightmare. It's every parent's worst nightmare, and it's really impossible for me to put into words what it feels like when you hear that news. You wanna die. You wanna not believe it, and the pain is just excruciating."

THIRTEEN

"She Hated Turtlenecks"

As the days wore on, the local Napa cops—supplemented by a lot of help—were still at the scene of the murders, trying to sort out exactly what had happened that night inside 2631 Dorset Street. The street remained blocked off, and men in white protective suits—state and federal forensic investigators—showed up to sift through every hair and fiber.

From an investigative standpoint, the Napa police department faced a big challenge: It had no weapon, no motive, and an ear-witness who saw a shape but nothing more. Everyone figured the intruder was a male, but even that wasn't yet established. There were not one but two victims, and there was the complicating factor that the murders—although they technically occurred on November 1—had taken place on Halloween night. Did someone driving by see the women handing out candy and take a shine to one of them? Had the killer deduced that only women lived there? Was it an attempted sexual assault? A ritualistic killing? The work of a cult? A jilted ex-boyfriend? A psycho who had seen Leslie compete in a beauty contest or had seen her photograph in a newspaper? So many questions, all without answers.

In the beginning, the police released very few details, and the rumors spread. People wondered if the murders had anything to do with the fact that Leslie worked at the Coppola winery. And since all three women had Italian-American surnames, people wondered if this could be the work of the mob. Some wondered suspiciously why Lauren had been spared. Others questioned whether one or more of the women were gay. The speculation was ludicrous, but everything was in play.

There was even talk that the infamous Zodiac killer had resurfaced. The serial killer terrorized San Francisco back in the 1960s and '70s and has never been captured, but area residents remembered that one of his most heinous attacks took place near Napa at Lake Berryessa

in September 1969, when he tied up and attacked a young couple with a knife, stabbing
them repeatedly and, according to the one who
survived, with relish. The murders of Adriane
and Leslie echoed that attack. Might Zodiac be
back in much the same way as the BTK (bind,
torture, kill) killer had resurfaced in Wichita,
Kansas?

But more than anything, the Napa community wanted information, and it desperately
wanted to know if the attack was targeted at one
or more of the women or if it was the work of
a serial killer. "People wanted to hear that the
killer was someone the girls knew," said Jeff
Schectman of KVON radio.

The news came out slowly. Napa's daily newspaper, the *Napa Valley Register*, was the conduit
between the populace and the police. The first
story did not even carry the names of the victims, but by Monday afternoon, November 1,
Kathleen Talbert, a spokeswoman for the Niebaum-Coppola winery, confirmed that one of
its workers, Leslie Mazzara, had been a victim.
Soon enough, Jay Shoemaker, CEO of the Coppola Companies, released this statement: "Leslie
Mazzara was part of the family of employees at
the Niebaum-Coppola Estate Winery. That she
made such an impact on all of us in the brief

time she was with us is a testament to her grace, charm, and generosity as a human being. The employees of the Niebaum-Coppola winery are deeply shocked and saddened by her loss. She has touched us all and will be sincerely missed. All of our sympathy goes out to her family, and if they can be comforted at all at this time, it would be knowing how much we will cherish the time we knew her."

The warm feelings for Leslie were genuine, according to a worker from the winery who asked to remain anonymous. "She was a sparkler, and everyone loved her, the workers here as well as the tourists who came into contact with her," the worker said.

But the employee admitted there was plenty of fear as well, because Leslie often partied with two other young women who worked at the winery—"They were really the babe squad"— and no one knew if the killer had targeted Leslie after seeing her at the winery or perhaps had seen all three women together at a restaurant or a bar. Tensions were high, and the good feeling of working at Coppola was gone, at least for the moment.

* * *

On Tuesday, November 2, autopsies of Adriane and Leslie were completed, and their identities officially were released to the public. Not surprisingly, both women died of multiple stab wounds, although it was clear Leslie had died quickly. "She did not have many stab wounds," Commander Troendly said. "[He] stabbed her right in the heart. She didn't have a chance." But that was not the case with Adriane, who had cuts and wounds on her upper body and arms. The frenzied stabbing convinced cops that this was a crime of rage, that the killer had to have known one or both of his victims. A relative who later saw Adriane's body said she had cuts between her fingers—defensive wounds that indicated she was trying to fight off her attacker. She also had a gash on her face and neck.

Some days later, she was dressed in a turtleneck in her coffin, a sight that struck her close friend Lily Prudhomme as especially odd. "Adriane never wore turtlenecks," Lily said. "She hated turtlenecks."

Friends and even those who had never met either young woman were devastated; it was a tragic story all the way around. But as news of the double murder spread beyond the Napa Valley, a cartoonish shorthand began popping up in the media: Leslie was "the beauty queen," and Adriane was "the local girl" or, worse, "the other roommate." Both families were upset with the headlines and the simplistic portrayal.

Both women, family and friends insisted, were so much more.

FOURTEEN

Adriane

Arlene Allen and her three daughters were well known in Calistoga, the small town at the northern end of the Napa Valley that is famous for its hot springs and mud baths. Some say you'll never relax as completely as you will sinking into a tub filled with mud and volcanic ash; others say you'll never be so disgusted in your entire life. Still, Calistoga and its mud baths have become synonymous, and the town's wide main street—Lincoln Avenue—retains a distinct western feel, not unlike Steamboat Springs in Colorado. Calistoga was founded by Samuel Brannon, who thought the hot springs and volcanic ash might make it a destination health resort as well known as Saratoga, New York. According to legend, Brannon declared the town would be the "Calistoga of Sarifornia" instead of the Saratoga of California. The name stuck.

The small-town atmosphere was attractive to Arlene. Raised in Killeen, Texas, when it had a population of 10,000, she loved the small-town way of living. "We used to catch corn toads in the creek beds and climb trees and have little adventures," she said. It was exactly what she wanted for her three girls, but at the time, she was living in Houston. Still, she was always searching for a place that would remind her of her own youth, and while on a vacation, she came upon Calistoga. "I thought, 'Wow, this is the place,' " she said. "This is a place where my kids can run and play and meet their neighbors."

She was in love with the area's beauty and small-town charm, and after she divorced her first husband, Tony Insogna, Adriane's father, she and her second husband, Peter Allen, moved to Calistoga in 1988. "It was the best decision I ever made," she said. It wasn't too long before Arlene and Peter were also divorced, but Arlene, a quiet woman who had always been able to draw on a well of inner strength, decided to make a stand. She stayed put, got a job as an office manager and accountant, became a board member of the Calistoga Joint Unified School

District, and raised her three girls—Lexi, Adriane, and Allison. Together they became a part of the community.

Adriane was the middle child and jokingly referred to as "the runt of the litter" by her mother and sisters. Arlene stands about five feet, nine inches, and her daughters Lexi and Allison are nearly six feet tall. Adriane was only five feet, six inches. Runt was, of course, a term of endearment.

"Adriane was, I think, your typical middle child," said Arlene. "She was very loving, very nurturing. When my youngest daughter was born, Adriane was only two and a half, and she became instantly attached to Allison, the youngest, and they just were a little twosome for the entirety of their childhoods. I used to refer to them as my Siamese twins joined at the hip. You never find one without the other. And Adriane always exhibited a loving spirit, and she always had this just wonderful smile on her face and sparkling blue eyes."

At the time of her death, Adriane was an assistant engineer at the Napa Sanitation District. It was a job she not only loved but seemed destined for from the time she was a young girl. Her favorite toy as a child was Lego, and she had what might be called an obsession with bridges.

Arlene said Adriane seemed to settle on her future sometime back in the eighth grade. "She was taking as an elective a mechanical drawing course. And it might've been the first or second week of school in her eighth grade when she came home and she said, 'You know, Mom, I think I want to do this the rest of my life.' And I recognized that something meaningful had just happened. So that was when we sat down together and explored various career possibilities that could entail that kind of work, and it was then that she settled on civil engineering."

Growing up in Calistoga, Adriane, like her sisters, was a joiner. She became a Brownie, then a Girl Scout, and proudly marched in the town's annual Fourth of July parade. "I still remember her carrying that big flag," Arlene said. "Boy, was it heavy."

Adriane loved the outdoors, a trait she retained throughout her too-short life. It was as a Girl Scout that Adriane met Amanda Miller, who was to become a lifelong friend. Miller, now Amanda Vaughan, laughed when she remembered those first childhood memories. "I actually remember Adriane way back when she had a Texan accent," she said. "We were in the same Girl Scout troop, Troop 258. On one of our first camping trips, they had us split into buttercup pairs. I was devastated as only a nine-year-old can be when I found myself odd man out among all my friends. I ran off and climbed to the top of one of the tallest trees, and no one was talking me down, or so I thought.

"Adriane was new to the troop, and she climbed all the way up that tree after me just to ask me to be her buttercup. After that, we were just inseparable, and she has been 'Buttercup' to me ever since."

It was a sweet gesture, one that Amanda never forgot. But that was Adriane. She enjoyed being involved. During her summers in high school, she and her classmates traveled to Mexico to build homes for those in need. More than one person described her as having a giving personality. But she also could be competitive and was even something of a jock. She loved sports and ran track and did the long jump, but volleyball became her passion. Adriane's life sounds idyllic, and it almost was—except for what her friends and family refer to as "the accident."

FIFTEEN

The Accident

"The accident" happened almost exactly ten years before Adriane was murdered. It was June 1994, and the school year had just ended at Calistoga High School. It was a day Arlene will never forget, the day Adriane borrowed her mother's 1981 Ford Thunderbird. "Adriane and Allison were home," Arlene recalled. "I called her from work and asked Adriane to run some errands for me in town and asked her to phone me back when she returned so I would know she had gotten back safe."

That call never came, and Arlene, figuring her daughter had just forgotten to call, as teenagers are prone to do, called home. She got Allison, not Adriane.

"Is your sister home?"

"Nope."

"Well, have you heard from her?"

"Nope."

"Do you know where she is?" Arlene asked, exasperated.

"Mom, am I her keeper? Do I know where she is every minute of the day? No. Why would you even think I would know?"

"Well, she took the car, so if you see her, have her call me at work right away."

Adriane didn't call, so Arlene headed home at her usual time, not thinking too much more of it except that she was going to reprimand Adriane for being scatterbrained. But as Arlene pulled her car into the driveway, she saw Allison standing there.

"Mom, the hospital called. Adriane's been in some kind of accident."

Arlene ran inside and reached a nurse, who told her, "Your daughter's been in an accident."

"Is she all right? How bad are her injuries?"

"Listen, Mrs. Allen, I think you should get here right away, but don't get into an accident yourself. Don't drive crazy. Just get here as soon as you can."

When Arlene and Allison got to the hospital and saw Adriane, they were devastated. Tubes were running everywhere, and her head had blown up to triple its normal size. It was clear she would need cosmetic surgery. Other parents were there of some boys who had also been in the accident, and after she calmed down, Arlene heard the story of what had happened.

"Adriane had met three boys from school while running her errands. These are boys who were not even in her class, boys she didn't hang out with, but for some reason, and I've never been able to ascertain what that reason was, she allowed one of them to drive her car.

"She did insist that they all wear seat belts. She was in the front passenger side, and there were two boys in the backseat, and then the driver. And they decided to drive down to the Napa Valley," Arlene said.

According to the police, an unnamed and unlicensed fifteen-year-old driving the car drifted onto a dirt shoulder on the side of the road and lost control as he tried to correct his maneuver. The car began a series of rolls.

"The car rolled at least three times," Arlene said. "And it was kind of an end-over-end, actually from the front passenger to the rear driver's side that it just rolled, and every time the car rolled, Adriane's head hit the pavement through the open window."

There was massive head trauma, and her life hung in the balance for a few days. Arlene couldn't look at her daughter without thinking of what she had looked like before the accident, and eventually, she brought a photograph to her bedside so the nurses could understand whom they were treating, the teenage girl beneath all the bandages. Arlene was heartbroken. "She had a gash that went from the middle of her cheek and went through and severed her ear on the right side. It was a very traumatic accident."

Her friend Amanda Vaughan remembered the accident and the injuries her close friend suffered. The doctors initially had thought she might not make it, but her will to live was strong. "It's amazing that Adriane made it through that accident as well as she did," Amanda said. "She had a slice along her face and through her ear. Luckily, a plastic surgeon was on duty, and he stitched her up so that you can barely tell."

But the healing process took a long time, and it was not just physical. "I thought that this accident was the worst thing that had ever happened," Arlene said. "But I didn't realize that the worst thing was just about to happen. And that is after Adriane returned home and after her injuries had healed on the outside, she returned to school. But she was still suffering temporary brain damage from the accident. And it was on a cognitive level.

"When she would read, she could read the words, but she couldn't tell you the gist of the paragraph that she just read. She had been a volleyball star who had been brought up to the varsity her sophomore year because of her talent, and here she was now beginning her junior year, and the coach was directing her, and she could not take the directions and turn them into actions.

"On top of that, the coach that year had a 'no excuses' policy, and Adriane couldn't even explain what the problem was. Her teammates began to make fun of her, you know, because of her mistakes that she was making on the court. You know, calling her a loser and various things. Her classmates ostracized her."

Adriane was in trouble on every level, and her grades began to slide downhill. "She had been an A student before," Arlene said. "And now she was really struggling with her schoolwork. And I was working very hard reading her assignments along with her so that we could then discuss them to make sure that she knew what was going on. Her world just got blacker and blacker. And what happened then was that she began to become very angry and bitter and hateful. And it really scared me, because this is nothing like the Adriane that I had known all these years."

Arlene asked Allison to keep an eye on Adriane at school, but, if anything, Arlene was even more shocked by what Allison reported. Adriane began to tell her friends that she wished she had died in the accident. Her mother was heartsick. "That really scared me. I knew she was depressed, but I didn't know it would be so bitter and dark, black even. She would get into arguments with even her closest friends for no reason. I knew she was at risk."

Adriane was already getting therapy, and she was on medication, but Arlene knew she needed something else, and oddly enough, that something else was a part-time job. "I recognized that all of her troubles were at school. And school was her entire world. And I thought that if she expanded her world to include other things, then she could gain self-esteem and feel good about herself in other areas, and then what was happening at school wouldn't be that important, wouldn't be as all-encompassing. Adriane always had a very strong work ethic. She went to work at a restaurant here in town."

The restaurant was Checkers, a casual eatery on Lincoln Avenue in downtown Napa, a salad and sandwich place where locals and tourists alike flock for a quick meal. There Adriane met Ron Golden, a very understanding boss.

"She immediately endeared herself to all of her coworkers and to her managers and to the owner of the restaurant by working hard, and before long she was her smiling self again. And within a few months, her brain damage disappeared. And by the end of that school year, she was back to her regular self," Arlene said.

The way Adriane fought back and came back against brain injuries was inspirational, and she was rewarded for all her hard work by an organization called If Given a Chance, which helps young people who overcome obstacles. It awarded Adriane a $2,500 annual scholarship to help her pay for the college of her choice, which happened to be Cal Poly, the California Polytechnic State University in San Luis Obispo, where, of course, she studied engineering. Not only was she studying exactly what she'd always hoped to, but her good friend Amanda was right there with her.

"Freshman year, we were chemistry lab partners at 8:00 in the morning," Amanda remembered, "and let me tell you, that's really early when you're a college student. We broke so much stuff while half-asleep in that class: crucibles, beakers, you name it. The worst was when we accidentally spilled liquid nitrogen on the computer cords. Thankfully, they thawed out just fine, and we both ended up with an A."

After college, the friends stayed in touch, but while Adriane got a job with the Napa Sanitation District and moved down to Napa, Amanda moved to Los Angeles, where she got a job and got married. Adriane told her about the great house she had and talked a lot about her roommate Leslie. "They were just two peas in a pod," Amanda said. "They hung out all the time. I met Leslie, and she was the sweetest thing ever with that Southern hospitality. It was a great household to be part of, and to tell the truth, I was a little jealous that she had such great friends living right with her. I couldn't have thought of a better place for Adriane to be; no one would have guessed about what was in store.

"She was safe; she was supposed to be safe. There's nothing that could have been done any differently, and it makes me angry. It makes me scared, because if she wasn't safe, then no one's safe."

Amanda cannot forget the worst day of her life. She had just come back from lunch, and a friend had sent her an e-mail that simply asked, "Are you there?"

She e-mailed her friend back: "Yeah, I'm doing fine, how are you?"

The response was unexpected: "Emergency, please call."

Amanda dialed but tried to calm herself. "I told myself, 'You're worrying for nothing. There's no big deal.'"

Amanda's friend, who still lived in Napa, answered the phone immediately: "Did you hear about the murder in Napa?"

"No, what happened?"

"Amanda, it was Adriane. She was killed."

"No, that can't be right. It must be a mistake. Are you sure? It can't be. It must be the wrong Adriane."

Amanda began poking around the Internet and found the news story. The names of the victims had not been released, but when she saw the street name, she said, "Then I knew. I've spent the night in that house."

Amanda remembers little else from that day. "I don't even know how I made it home. It was hard to believe that anyone would want to actually hurt Adriane."

Since then, Amada said, "there's a huge hole in my life. Initially, I felt like the world was gonna end, and then it didn't. And I just kind of played along. It doesn't seem right. Adriane is supposed to be here. I guess, looking back, that maybe I took her for granted a little because everywhere I look, I'm reminded of her. I didn't realize she was intertwined in my life so tightly until she was gone. She was my one friend who was also a girl engineer; those are very rare.

"You just have to concentrate on the good, or else you'll be sad forever. The only time I cry now is when I drive and I have nothing to keep me occupied; that's when I start thinking about Adriane, the little things, the facial expressions."

It was a small thing, but Amanda didn't know what to do about her makeup in the weeks after the murder, because it was Adriane who used to sell it to her. Six months before she died, Adriane had become a Mary Kay saleswoman, "and now all my products are running out, and it's just another reminder that she's not here; she was so many things to me. Some days, I forget she's not here anymore, and I think, 'Oh, I've gotta tell Adriane this. I haven't been able to take her number off my phone or off my e-mail list. And every now and then, I see there she is. And I wanna call her, forward her a joke on e-mail or instant-message her.

"I stare at her screen name, waiting for it to light up and say that she's online. I would do anything to have her back."

SIXTEEN

A Huge Puzzle

On Wednesday, November 3, the top brass of the Napa police department decided to show their hand just a bit. Some important evidence had come back from the forensics lab, and it was time to let the community in on it. First off, the police revealed that whoever had killed Adriane and Leslie had been injured and bled in the house. They had the killer's DNA, and one thing was for sure: the killer was a male.

It was a major break. The police quickly entered the DNA into the state database to see if they would get a hit from someone with a prior record, whether it was a sexual predator, a killer, or even a burglar. There were no positive hits, but the DNA was still important. Anyone who became a suspect would be asked to provide a DNA sample—it only required passing a cotton swab along the inside of someone's cheek—and if they matched, the cops would have their killer. Of course, investigations are never that easy, and the Napa cops didn't expect this one to be, either. Still, if someone refused a DNA test, that person would get a second look.

Commander Jeff Troendly, short and muscular, with a shaved head, was in charge of speaking to the media in addition to leading the investigations bureau. He's a friendly sort who is good at his job, too good for the reporters working the case, actually. Troendly would let out only the information the cops wanted to get out and nothing more. "The DNA evidence acts as a genetic fingerprint and will help us identify and eliminate potential suspects," Troendly said. "At this time, we do not have a preliminary suspect or a motive."

The public was told to watch neighbors and coworkers carefully; it was clear the killer had been injured. Troendly asked the public to take notice of unexplained scratches and bandages, or perhaps the killer had called in sick to work the day after the murders. And there was more, other genetic material collected from the house—Troendly refused to say what it was—

and the cops were waiting for that to come back from the lab. They had high hopes that, with the public's help, they might catch a break. "We only have one sample back from the lab," Troendly said. "But as time goes on and we get more lab results, there could be more suspects. We just don't know."

Although the Napa police department was getting assistance from the FBI and the state, they immediately set up their own seven-man investigative unit with one supervisor to do the day-to-day investigative work. Based on how quick and vicious the attack was and how the killer bypassed Lauren Meanza to go directly up the stairs, the investigative team felt the killing spree was not random but targeted, directed at one of the two dead women. It still would be a few days before they would release that information to the general public, but they felt sure it was the right way to go about the investigation.

That approach placed a structure on the overall investigation and meant, for starters, that the unit would collect DNA samples from all the men who had dated or were close to the victims. The police decided they would start with the inner circle of friends and relatives of the women and work out from there, going after those who had less and less daily contact with the housemates. Before long, they even were collecting DNA from neighbors. "You always want to find out who they are dating or who did they just wind up breaking up with, because a lot of crimes we deal with are crimes related to crimes of passion, spurned lovers, things like that," Detective Todd Shulman said. "We're always going to start at the very most interpersonal relationships we can with the victim. It's the closest people in their lives. When you're dealing with a young, single girl, that could be someone they're dating, a boyfriend, or an ex-boyfriend."

Shulman seemed particularly interested in Leslie's past. "That was a woman who was a very active young lady who was brand new to California, basically trying to find herself and find her way in a new career and a new city," he said. "She was very social, very outgoing, very friendly. She had a lot of relations with a lot of people both here and back in the South where she was from."

There was a persistent rumor that Leslie had left South Carolina after a bad breakup, and Shulman was determined to flesh out that lead. "He is a person of interest. That was her last serious relationship before coming out here. We want to find out his feelings toward Leslie," the cop said.

"This is a very complex investigation," Troendly said. "We have this huge puzzle and all the pieces are still spread everywhere. These women had numerous friends, numerous contacts. It could be any one of hundreds of people, perhaps even thousands."

Of course, as the Napa detectives knew, just because the attack seemed to be targeted, it did not mean either of the dead women *knew* her attacker. There was always the possibility that a stalker had fixated on one of them and decided, for whatever reason, that Halloween was the best time to act. The zip ties found at the scene were another important clue: it seemed as though the attacker had entered the house with the intention of tying up one or maybe all three of the women, possibly to sexually assault them. Had they awakened and attacked him before he had that chance? The possibilities were vast. The cops needed help, and they knew it.

Because the Napa police had so few officers, it was decided that some recent retirees would be rehired to help in the investigation. One of those was Detective Dan Lonegan, who had left the force back in 2002. "I'm not a savior by any means," said the affable Lonegan. "But I did a lot of interviews over the years, and I dealt with a lot of people. You get what they call a sixth sense of people after a while. It doesn't work all the time, but you do get a lot of experience that way."

Lonegan grew up in the Napa Valley in the 1940s and was in the third generation in his family to be raised there. He's old enough to remember when Napa was "a meat-and-potatoes town . . . but then the wine industry took off and the whole culture and everything changed. Used to be pretty down-to-earth, but now it's a lot more sophisticated. When I was growing up, nobody ever heard of Napa Valley. The wine industry was here, but nothing like it is now."

The nature of Napa would be important to the investigation, because it had become a town full of transients and visitors, one of whom may have had something to do with this crime. If that was the case, this was going to be a very tough crime to solve.

"It could be somebody's next-door neighbor. It could be someone who lives a nine-to-five life. Has a family, wife, kids, and has a normal job. Maybe they got caught up in a relationship or maybe they fixated on one of these women, and it just got out of control."

Figuring out the motive of the killer meant

learning as much as they could about the victims.

Learning about Adriane's past was relatively easy, since she was local, but to know more about Leslie, they'd have to travel 3,000 miles east to Anderson, South Carolina.

SEVENTEEN

The New Baby

By the time Cathy Harrington gave birth to her daughter, Leslie, she had just turned twenty-seven and already had two sons: PJ, who was then nine years old, and Andy, five. The household had a decidedly masculine, rambunctious tilt. Cathy can laugh about it now, but she wasn't laughing back then. "My sons were always being mean to each other," she says. "They were always wrestling on the floor and beating each other up. They were always in a tumble on the floor, and I just thought they were gonna be uncivilized savages when they grew up. I thought I had to be the worst mother in the world.

"And then Leslie was born, and I saw this other side of them. I mean, they were just immediately fascinated with this beautiful little baby. And they were so sweet to her. I thought, 'Oh, my God, there's hope.' So Leslie really blessed our lives."

Those were very tough years for Cathy, a spiritual woman who seemed trapped by the rash decisions of youth. She was only eighteen years old when she became a mother to PJ. He and Andy have the same father, but Leslie's dad, Lenny Mazzara, was out of the picture quickly. "I was divorced when Leslie was four days old," Cathy says. "And suddenly I was on my own with these three little kids."

It was that way most of the time Leslie was growing up. There was no one constant male figure in her mother's life. She was on her own in a small house in a rural farming area just outside Anderson. Of course, Cathy loved her sons, but, as she will tell you, there's something different about the bond between a mother and a daughter. Leslie became the joy of her life, her real-life "Princess," which became her nickname. "She made it easy for me to get up and go to work and try to survive. She had a crib at the edge of my bed, and her first word was 'Hi.' And I would wake up in the morning, she'd be standing there looking over at me, and she'd say, 'Hi.' And you couldn't be depressed or feel sorry for yourself when you have this joyous little creature. She gave me a reason to get up and go to work. She came into this world with this warmth and life. Leslie was happy, and when she was tiny, I wrote her a song."

The song is called "Leslie's Lullaby," and its lyrics include: "Precious little one, you spread warmth greater than the sun . . . special little one, I must express in song, my gratitude to the one above for he chose me to be the one."

It's a sweet song, and Anderson, South Carolina, where they lived, is a sweet place to live, the quintessential small Southern town. Located in the northern part of the state, it is overshadowed by its much bigger cousins, Atlanta to the south and Charlotte to the north. It reminds one of the Michael J. Fox film *Doc Hollywood,* where Fox, an aspiring cosmetic surgeon bound for Los Angeles to make his fortune, stumbles into a tiny Southern town that he finds is long on charm——but only after he loses the big-city attitude and pays attention. Anderson is probably not as small as Grady was in the film, but it feels that way. Its nickname is "The Friendliest City in South Carolina," but it's a way station, and those who stay are likely to have been born there or have kin nearby.

Cathy's life with three young children, however, was anything but a movie. It was a struggle, pure and simple. She dreamed of being a songwriter, and, like in a country song, life was dragging her down. "I would do everything in my power to give Leslie all she needed," Cathy said. "When she was just a baby, I got a grant to go to school to study at a community college. I was a hairdresser, but I got a grant, so I went. And I was working part-time and taking music classes and English 101. I was going to get a degree, and then the gas company turned my gas off because I couldn't pay an $18 bill. We were living in poverty for a lot of those years when I was a single mom. Barely making it. Barely putting food on the table. And when the gas company turned off my gas, we had to heat water in a skillet."

Cathy worked mostly as a hairdresser, and with her own shock of thick, curly red hair, she knows a thing or two about unruly hair. "I was making $150 a week take-home, and my child-care bill was $85 a week, so I couldn't pay rent and all the bills and food and everything on top of that. So after one semester, I realized that if it was right for me to go to school, it would be working out better. So that's when I quit school, and there was a real sadness for me to have to give up that dream, but that was also a time when I really understood what it is to be a mother and to give my children everything.

"I also didn't want to look back and say, 'I wish I had done this or that differently.' If they didn't turn out good, then I could always look back and go, 'I did the best I could. It's not my fault. I did the best I could.' And so I did that. I just threw myself into being their mom."

She joked that she could always save money on cutting their hair. "I even started entering contests cutting hair, and I won awards for it, too," she said.

One thing that Cathy is especially proud of and has pointed to after the murder was something that Leslie said to a judge at the 2002 Miss South Carolina contest. Leslie's good buddy Kelly McCorkle won the whole shebang, but Leslie won the interview section. A tape exists of the interview, and in it Leslie tells the judge, "We came from a family where we all knew we were loved."

That brings tears to Cathy's eyes.

"We were very lucky," Cathy said. "And her brothers were just crazy about her. I remember one time . . . I never spanked her because she was so good. But one day she was doing something she shouldn't have, and she was about three, and I just swatted her on the leg. Well, it just threw her into hysterics, because she didn't know what that was all about. And she went into her brothers' room, crying. And I heard Andy say, 'Baby, what's the matter?' and she said, 'Mother.' And so Andy comes out with his hands on his hips, and he says, 'All right, who hit her?' I mean, that's the way they were with her. Yet they would do terrible things to her. Like they learned to make a noose in Boy Scouts, and they'd hang her dolls from trees and rig them up to hear her scream and tease her. But they adored her, and she knew it. She was very lucky to have big brothers."

Cathy admitted that she and her sons spoiled Leslie, and her old friend Kelly saw proof of that the first time Leslie stayed over at Kelly's house. "My mom said, 'Girls, you can't leave until Kelly's done the dishes.' And Leslie goes, 'You have to do the dishes?' She could not believe it. It didn't take me long to realize that she truly was a princess."

EIGHTEEN

Leslie

If there's one thing everyone says about Leslie, it's that she was a happy person who had the ability to make others happy. To hear her friends speak of her, it's almost as though they are talking of a deity who walked among us. What they say goes far beyond the typical platitudes one might offer up for a woman who died tragically and far too young. It's clear that Leslie must have had a sunny personality, because everyone says the same thing: that she could walk into a room and hold everyone's attention. She was friendly, personable, and loads of fun. People liked to be with her. As one friend said, "Women wanted to be her, and men wanted to be with her."

That began probably from birth and was evident throughout her childhood. Maybe it comes from having two older brothers who lavished her with attention. "At nursery school, they told me that Leslie gave everybody happy lessons. She had a special way of making people feel that same love. She would reflect love to people, and they were drawn to that," Cathy said. "She had sort of a bright energy, a very special energy."

Leslie's passion for dance was partly how she won the Miss Williamston crown. It began when she was five, when she taught her school chums how to dance to one particular song. When her mother saw what Leslie had taught them, she became alarmed. "She was too good at those sultry moves," Cathy said, "and I thought to myself, 'I need to get her some classical ballet classes.' So we went strictly classical, and she had amazing training."

She was so good she was asked to take classes each summer in the prestigious Governor's School for the Arts, which is where she met Kelly McCorkle. Later the two of them went to live in New York City for a summer, where they both studied with the Alvin Ailey dance company. New York pushed the women hard, and they pushed back. Kelly got mononucleosis and was unable to attend a lot of the classes. Another time, she was followed home by a stalker who chased her until she broke free and called the police. Leslie was protective and told her they were not going out for a long time.

But they also had fun and came away with some funny stories. A neighbor baked Leslie a strawberry shortcake for her birthday on August 1, but the woman had a very small New York kitchen and often blow-dried her hair near the stove. As Leslie and Kelly were eating the cake, Kelly noticed a hair, but that didn't stop Leslie, who kept right on eating and said, "I don't care. It tastes too darned good."

The women scrimped on food, eating Ramen noodles every day, and used all their cash for clothes. They came up with a silly little song that is decidedly not politically correct. It's called the "Anorexic Song," and Kelly still remembers that the lyrics went something like this "I wanna be an anorexic, nothing but skin and bones. I wanna be a bulimic, regurgitate ice cream cones. Sometimes I eat, Sometimes I don't, but when I do, it comes back up my throat."

And that reminds her friends and family of another Leslie story, of the time she made a national television appearance. "When she was getting ready to leave New York, she told me she was gonna get on the David Letterman show. By God, she did," said Kelly.

It's true. Just scoring tickets to the Letterman show is tough enough, but Leslie went one better. Her engaging personality even caught the often-jaded eye of Letterman. During an audience warm-up, Leslie chatted up Letterman by telling him her Grammy had gone to Ball State University, Letterman's alma mater. When the taping renewed after the break, Letterman pointed to Leslie and pulled her out of the audience to go out onto the street with a professional soccer player for a typically crazy stunt. While the soccer player bounced a ball endlessly on his head, Leslie sat nearby in a lawn chair and watched. But the mere fact that Leslie set out to be on the show and then achieved it was something else to family and friends. "*That* was pretty amazing," Cathy said.

Her mother always knew that Leslie had a great sense of humor and remembers that even when she was only twelve, she could crack everyone up. "We had gone to see a Jackson Browne concert, and I was with my friends Dale and Elizabeth, and we had just come from a restaurant having dinner," she said. "Leslie and I were walking side-by-side in front of Dale and Elizabeth, and Dale said, 'Cathy, you and Leslie look just alike.' And Leslie, without missing a beat, said, 'Mom, Dale just said I have a big butt.' She was really good with those, and quick as well."

Sometimes she could be too good, such as when she demonstrated how her brothers taught her to belch loudly and often. And PJ and Andy never did stop teasing her completely, as Cathy recalled: "When she won the Miss Williamston pageant, they called her 'Miss Possum Kingdom' because it was such a small town."

Life changed for Cathy and Leslie when Leslie turned eighteen and was getting ready to attend the University of Georgia. Cathy's sons were off living on their own, and for the first time in a long time, Cathy felt free. She'd always been a restless soul, and she decided it was time to get back to doing things for herself. Egged on by a friend, she decided it would be a good idea to go to Alaska and open up a bakery called the Miller's Daughter. Cathy took off, leaving Leslie in the care of Grammy, Judy Harrington.

"I had been a mother since I was eighteen, and I was so ready to do my own thing," Cathy said. "It was only later I realized how hard it was for Leslie at eighteen years old for her mother to move to Alaska while she was in college."

Leslie did sorely miss her mother, and for three consecutive summers, she would visit Cathy in Alaska. "She worked in the bakery, and she made really good use of her Southern accent and her charming good looks. She wowed everybody in Alaska, and she had a wonderful time," Cathy said.

Childhood friend Amy Brown joined her one summer and they both worked at the bakery from 5:30 a.m. to 1:00 p.m. "And then we'd go have fun," Amy said. The two did endless hiking with a variety of men who were drawn to the good-looking girls with the Southern drawls. "We were known as the Miller's Daughters," Amy said. "We had a lot of fun. We were wearing tank tops and shorts and standing on top of snow. It was a blast."

Amy, who spoke to Leslie almost every day right up to the end of her life, admitted that Leslie did have one bad habit: she was a slob when it came to leaving her clothes all over her room. "When you walked into her room, it was nothing but a sea of clothes," Amy said. "They were everywhere, on the bed, on the floor. Nothing was hanging up in the closet. And what was amazing is, she could tell me where everything was. She said, and I quote, 'The pink shirt should be under the green pants to the right of my blue jeans. And my black skirt is under the bed, left of the flip-flops.' And to my surprise, there they were. Now, that's talent."

Amy got married just weeks before Leslie's

murder, and Leslie traveled back east to be in the wedding party. "PJ, her brother, asked my husband if he knew that he was marrying both of us. It was just that simple."

The relationship was symbiotic, Amy said, laughing. "She taught me how to eat and flirt and I taught her how to hang a ceiling fan and how to shoot a layup."

Amy paused for a moment, as she often did when speaking of her friend; a look passed across her eyes as though she just realized Leslie was dead. "I was with Leslie for such a long time that I don't know who I am," she said, crying.

Leslie often lived in Amy's house when the two were not in school and even later in life. Amy had two dogs, Tucker and Cody. "I always ran with Tucker and Amy ran with Cody. We'd run side-by-side with our Walkmen on . . ." She trailed off. "We both loved animals."

The day Leslie won the Miss Williamston contest and her own tiara, Cathy was in Berkeley studying for the ministry. "It's one of the great regrets I have, that I wasn't able to be there," Cathy said. According to friends, it did cause Leslie some pain, but, in typical Leslie fashion, she never truly let on to her mother, instead never letting her forget she missed the big event by making her mother's absence into a joke. "When she called me up, she'd say, 'Whatcha doin', Mommy?' " Cathy recalled. "And I said, 'Oh, I'm writing a paper. What are you doing?' And she'd say, 'I'm doing my laundry with my tiara on.' "

Sometime after winning the title, Leslie gave a joke gift to her mom for Christmas. It was a photo of Leslie with her tiara on her head, and there was a little button to press. "She recorded a message, and when I push it, I hear her voice still," Cathy said. "It makes me laugh so hard. It's a line from one of Leslie's favorite movies, *Steel Magnolias*. She almost knew the movie by heart, and what she recorded in this picture was, 'There's no such thing as natural beauty.' It's so funny! Oh, I laugh so hard when I hear that. That was her favorite movie. Well, her other favorite movie was *Shadowlands*."

"And *Beaches*," Andy said.

"And *Beaches*! Oh, my gosh, she had a lot of favorite movies, didn't she?"

It took Leslie—and Amy—seven years to graduate from college, and when she did, she left with a philosophy major. Cathy said, "I don't remember how many majors she had, ten maybe. What do you do with a degree in philosophy?"

Cathy didn't know, and neither did Leslie.

She worked in a law office as a paralegal for a while but grew bored, and when she broke up with the man she was living with, she decided it was time to have an adventure of her own. After her mother invited her to California, her brother Andy suggested she try to get a job at the Nie-baum-Coppola winery. He'd visited the winery on a previous trip and was impressed.

In no time, Leslie had a job there. It all seemed so easy, but it was not long before Cathy was on the move again. No sooner had Leslie turned up than Cathy got a job as a minister in Ludington, Michigan. But Leslie stayed put, and her family knew why: she had found her niche and seemed glad to be away from the East Coast and away from a relationship that had turned sour.

"She was probably the happiest I've ever seen her," Cathy said. "She was in her element. The princess was living in elegance and working in elegance and having the opportunity to really shine and be appreciated for all her gifts, so it's a comfort to know that she was happy.

"She called me a lot, and the first thing she would say is, 'Hi, Mommy.' And when we would hang up, she'd always end it with, 'I sure do love you, Mommy.'

"I miss that, but I still hear it in my head, and in my head I remember her."

NINETEEN

"We Need Your Help"

While the investigations into the lifestyle and friends of Adriane and Leslie continued at full speed, Napa's new police chief began a campaign to ease the public's mind. Chief Rich Melton had been in the city and at the top job for only two months after coming over from Los Alamos, and he had a big-time crisis on his hands. He didn't need anyone to tell him that the law-abiding citizens of Napa were upset and needed to be placated. On Saturday, November 6, Melton called a community meeting to give Napans an update on the investigation. More than five hundred residents—some curious, some angry—packed the multipurpose room at Harvest Middle School.

It seemed as though everyone had a question, and most wanted reassurances from the cops that this attack was not a random act of violence. The cops onstage—Melton, along with Commanders Steve Potter and Jeff Troendly—told the assembled that the police believed the killer had targeted one or both of the women. "It's our belief," Melton told the audience, "that this was a directed attack. There are very specific reasons we believe that. We aren't just trying to tell you something to try and make you feel good. We want to be as forthcoming as we can, but we don't want to do anything that will damage this case. We are working this case for a successful prosecution."

One curious moment occurred when a resident demanded to know if Lauren Meanza was being considered a suspect. "Right now, that's not where we are headed," Melton said.

According to a witness, one woman, when she heard that, stalked out of the auditorium muttering about there being something wrong with "that girl." It should be noted that at this stage, there was a lot of talk about what Lauren did and did not do on the night of the murders. People were curious about how she had escaped and why she got out with not a scratch on her while her roommates had been so viciously stabbed over and over. No doubt, if she were a man, she'd be the number one suspect. Did she have some type of agenda against the others? Was there a connection that the cops were hiding? They insisted this was not so, but Lauren's behavior was raising eyebrows all over town. Sentences that began with "No one knows what they would do in that position, but . . ." were frequently heard. And one close friend of the women said he went to see Lauren at her parents' home two days after the attack, but she was out. Her folks said she had gone to volleyball practice. "She seemed strangely unaffected," the friend said, "though it could be she was in shock."

It was noted over and over, almost as an excuse, that Lauren was "quiet" and not as social as Adriane and Leslie. People were curious, but Lauren was under wraps and, at that point, not talking to anyone but the police. The full story of what had happened in the house remained a mystery even to the families of Adriane and Leslie.

Deanna Bevans, a neighbor of the young women on Dorset Street, told the *Napa Valley Register,* "they weren't party girls, they were very nice girls," and mentioned that Adriane had brought her three daughters Halloween cupcakes a few days before the murders. Bevans, who had recently moved to Napa from Oregon, said the murders were causing her to rethink her move, and she was clearly terrified that the killer might strike again. Anyone in her position, with three young daughters, would have been crazy not to be concerned. She told the *Register* she had installed new locks and an alarm system but still did not feel safe. "I'm devastated, I'm scared, I can't sleep," she said. "I don't know what to do."

Melton continued his familiar refrain. The public could help solve this crime if they paid attention to those around them. If the killer was one of them, he would be behaving nervously, he would have his daily patterns disrupted, he might have some unexplained scratches, possibly on his face. "What we are asking is help from the community," the chief said. "Most crimes are solved on things people tell the police."

A day later, the police held another meeting, this time at the St. John the Baptist Church right after a Spanish-speaking mass. About 350 Latinos were in the audience, and the meeting was held because the police were concerned that the crowd at the Harvest Middle School did not represent a true cross-section of the population. The unspoken message was that perhaps the killer was a Latino grape picker and the police wanted to be sure that this population also was looking for any suspicious behavior by one of their own.

"We need to incorporate all of the community to help," Melton said. "It's very important for us to get all the information that we can to help solve the murders."

Now the word was out, but would the police be getting anything back?

TWENTY

Goodbye, Buttercup

One week and a day after the murders of Adriane Michelle Insogna and Leslie Ann Mazzara, it was time for their families and friends to say goodbye. No one had yet been caught, but now was not the time to dwell on that cruel fact. It was Tuesday, November 9, and this was Adriane's day, the day she would be buried at the age of twenty-six, the first of the victims to be laid to rest.

Adriane's funeral took place at the Community Presbyterian Church in Calistoga. Her mother, Arlene Allen, and her two sisters, Allison and Lexi, were joined by Adriane's father, Tony Insogna, his second wife, Kay, and their son, Michael. The day matched the mood: it was overcast as some four hundred mourners formed a long, solemn line waiting their turn to enter the small church. There wasn't room for everyone, and those who could not fit inside stood outside on the lawn and listened through a loudspeaker. Nearly everyone was crying, especially Adriane's father, Tony, who told family members that he was desperately sorry he'd missed seeing Adriane grow into the woman she became. The geographic distance from Texas and the psychic distance from his first wife, Arlene, had made him an absent father. He'd always thought there would be time to get to know her, and now the time had run out. He was inconsolable.

Also there was Peter Allen, Adriane's stepfather. He, too, remembered her love of bridges and said, "It's a bad day, of course. Adriane was such a great kid. We really want her to be remembered as she was alive, not at this moment here."

Not many knew it, but Napa detectives circulated among the news photographers and cameramen, handing out their business cards and asking them to hold on to their stills and video in case the killer was wandering among the mourners. When and if he was finally identified, the cops wanted to check if he'd been there.

Rev. David Moon-Wainwright officiated and

tried to comfort the mourners by putting the best spin he could on Adriane's murder. "We don't know what really happened in those last few minutes of Adriane's life, but we do know she was responding out of love for her friend and her other friend who was downstairs," he said. "There were so many people's lives that were touched by Adriane, so many of those people have come to say goodbye. We not only have come to cry but celebrate, because she is beyond death and at peace in God's arms."

One by one, Adriane's family, friends, and coworkers selected their memories of her. Loyal friend Amanda, who had nicknamed Adriane "Buttercup" when they'd met in the Girl Scouts, said, "Adriane always took the effort to stay in touch when we graduated and went off to college. When I heard the news of her death, I was just hoping it was a different Adriane, but when they said the house was on Dorset Street, I knew. I've been to that house, and I knew Adriane's bedroom was upstairs."

Adriane's aunt, Penny Embry, also spoke. "Everyone who knew my sister's daughter will know that Adriane is a great and loving spirit, and her gestures were never empty or self-serving. Everybody in this building will have heard these words a thousand times."

"She was everything you would want in a friend," Kara Mullinix, a friend, said through tears.

Vickie Sermas, Adriane's high-school volleyball and basketball coach, agreed. She told the *Napa Valley Register,* "Adriane was always so supportive. She just wanted what was best for everyone else. She was so into her family, always looking out for her sisters. She was just a great person."

Todd Herrick, who worked in the small offices of the Napa Sanitation District with Adriane, tried to lighten the mood just a bit. "Her coworkers and I decided we would try to make a list of things that Adriane liked and disliked, but she was such a positive person, we decided to make a list of Adriane's likes and loves," he said. "She liked her two-seater Geo convertible that leaked, but she loved her 4Runner she worked so hard and saved to buy. She liked to go to job sites wearing her orange vest and blue steel-toed shoes. She loved those shoes. Adriane just never had a bad day at work."

Ron Golden, the owner of Checkers restaurant, who hired Adriane to bus tables when she was at her lowest point in high school, recovering from her car crash injuries and battling depression, said, "Even after she graduated and went on to college, she would come home for the summers and work at the restaurant. People always say when someone dies that the victim would have done anything for anyone, but that's really the truth about Adriane. She always cared more about others than she cared about herself."

The one person who did not speak was Adriane's mom, Arlene, who was too overcome. She had been leaning for support on Jeff Johnson, the superintendent of the Calistoga Unified School District. He'd been fielding media calls for her, including those from *48 Hours,* and he spoke for Arlene at this, her lowest point. "The family is grieving," Johnson said, "but Arlene said she is comforted by all the support the community has shown her and her family. They moved here to Calistoga from Texas about seventeen years ago, and she practically raised her children as a single mom. It's a very difficult time for all of them. Adriane was so very close to her family."

As the funeral ended and the mourners dispersed, the rains began, and Adriane was taken from Calistoga one last time to be buried in a private service in the Knight's Valley cemetery. Later that day, there was a postfuneral reception at a local Calistoga restaurant. A griefstricken Arlene Allen was the center of attention as a line of people waited to speak to her and give her whatever words of solace they could muster.

"Arlene is such a nice woman," said Ben Katz, a friend of Adriane's. "She talked to every single person there, and her plate of food sat in front of her untouched."

That evening, Adriane's two sisters, Lexi and Allison, and five friends climbed into a stretch limo to remember their friend. Along for the ride was Ben Katz, Christian Lee, Lily Prudhomme, Derek Santiago, and Lexi's husband, Rob. The ride went by in a blur of tears and emotions. They stopped at a bar or two in and around Santa Rosa but mostly kept to themselves inside the limo. "It seemed like we all knew different sides of Adriane, and we told about how we remembered her," said Derek.

Initially, Ben said he was suspicious of both Christian and Derek, whom he had never met, but after seeing how Adriane's sisters treated them, he came around and dropped his guard. It was a long, booze-filled night of emotions that needed to be let out. The friends all promised to stay in touch and consoled each other. Derek had already been questioned by detectives, who asked for his DNA and had had him remove his shirt to see if he had any scratches on his back. He had spoken to Adriane about a week before the murder, and all she could talk about was how excited she was to be going to Australia with Lily on November 25.

The limo ride was a release from all the pent-up tension and sadness, and too soon, it seemed, it was time for the friends to say their goodbyes. "The one image I have in my mind is how distraught Lily was," Derek said. "When we pulled up to let her off, I had my arm around her because she was crying so hard."

As Lily stepped out of the car, she said, "How could someone do this? How could someone take her from us?"

If there was one small consolation in the aftermath of Adriane's death, Lily knew it was that her relationship with her boyfriend, Eric, had grown stronger and more stable. He was there for her the moment she stepped out of the limo, consoling her when she walked through the door of the apartment they shared.

TWENTY-ONE

Grief Constricts You

The day Adriane Insogna was buried, Leslie's mother, Cathy, was doing something no mother should ever have to do. She was shopping to buy a new dress for her only daughter's funeral. "It was the last time I could shop for her. I bought her a necklace and earrings and a suit from Casual Corner, a petite. I kept remembering what she always said to me: for an interview suit, you should always have a navy blue suit. So I bought a really attractive navy blue suit."

The moments around the death of a loved one stand out forever in time. One remembers the little details, and this was no exception. And so it is for Cathy, who cannot shake the thought of the saleswoman who sold her Leslie's last dress. Cathy knew she was a nice woman who was just trying her hardest, but everything the woman said turned out to be wrong. "She kept telling me to save the receipts, because then she could bring it back." Cathy didn't have the heart to tell her the horrid truth.

When it came time to pick out a final resting place for Leslie, PJ did most of the planning. She was to be placed in a mausoleum, because he and Andy could not bear the thought of their sister being buried. And they made sure there would be room there for Leslie's beloved Grammy, who, in a sad twist of fate, would now follow her granddaughter someday. Cathy picked out the casket and made sure it had angels on both sides, because, she explained, "Leslie was our angel."

Life without Leslie was almost unbearable for Cathy. "At first, every day I got up, I had to make the choice of whether I wanted to live or if I just wanted to die. But we must choose life. Leslie taught that. She taught life and living and enjoying, sharing, connecting with people."

And the connections Leslie made turned out to be intense, in death as they were in life. Her car insurance salesman sent Cathy a note, and when Cathy told the saleswoman who had leased Leslie her car what had happened and why she was returning the car, the woman burst into tears. "She had only the briefest contact with Leslie, but she remembered her vividly," Cathy said.

She knew she was a different person from the one who had been "called" by her Michigan congregation. Cathy had just graduated from the seminary and was to have been ordained on November 14, 2004, at a ceremony Leslie had planned to attend. Now, her only daughter would not be there, and the pain was crushing. Leslie's death was the painful fulfillment of a premonition she'd had when she was much younger. Cathy had always feared that something terrible would happen, she said, to her. "So I decided that I would do good things and keep something bad from happening. I started volunteering at a home for handicapped adults, giving them haircuts. And I took Leslie there with me many times, just trying to find ways to earn my keep in this world, to bless the world so that I wouldn't wait until tragedy happened before I did that, so when this happened, I felt like I'd already paid the piper. It's not fair. What more was I supposed to do? But the only way I can look at it is that we had Leslie for twenty-six years. She was a gift, an amazing gift. And I would do it again tomorrow, even if I knew the outcome."

She stopped and then said, "But I can't find any meaning yet.

"I think that love doesn't die and that energy doesn't die and that Leslie is a beautiful light. There's no way her light can be gone. It's here, it's with us. C. S. Lewis says that when you're in grief, it's like fear. It constricts you, and there's no room for anything else, but as time passes and the grief eases a little, then you can feel the person with you as more than a memory, as an actual experience of them."

Cathy was grateful to be wrapped in the arms of others. The day of the funeral, about three hundred people showed up at the Sullivan-King Mortuary's northeast chapel to remember Leslie back in her hometown of Anderson, South Carolina, where they heard Rev. Tom Ritchie remind them to think of Leslie's life as a series of "happiness lessons."

But sadness and regret were the order of the day. Most recalled that Leslie always had said she wanted to get married and have four sons. And her husband had to look like the writer John Grisham. "She was always searching for the perfect mate, and now I feel cheated," Cathy said. "I feel really cheated because she was my only daughter, and we had all the mother-daughter things growing up. I just adored her, and we went through all of these good and bad times together, and at age twenty-six, she and I were best friends. It's so unfair that I can't go through all the rest of her life with her, to hold her babies when they first come on the earth and to be with her when she got married. It's just not fair."

Everyone goes through grief with different emotions in different ways. For Leslie's brother Andy, it was the "dreams" he kept having on and off. In one, he kept trying to get to 2631 Dorset Street but could not get there in time. "Just trying to be there so I can warn her, just trying to get to her," he said quietly.

"The hardest thing for me now is that I still see her face in the crowd when I'm walking through the mall or something, and I stop and look twice. I think, 'There's my sister's face I just saw on somebody,' and then I think no. I'm still coming to the realization that she's gone for me, but still, when I see someone who reminds me of my sister, it all comes back to me again," he said.

For Amy Brown, the loss of Leslie was felt in little, day-to-day things, things that bond women in ways men often don't understand. "It's not like we did special things on special days,"

Amy said. "We lived our lives together. That's not replaceable. I miss her advice. I miss calling her to make a decision on what color of lipstick I should buy."

She remembered one typical conversation that meant nothing and everything at the same time.

"Leslie, I'm in Target, and I've got this peach lipstick and more of a mocha lipstick and I don't know which I should buy. What do you think?"

"Well," Leslie would say. "What are you wearing right now?"

Amy would describe her clothing, and then Leslie would say, "Well, you know, I kinda think you should get the mocha because you're a little bit darker, so I think you should just go ahead and go with that."

"We'd have those types of conversations all the time," Amy said. "It was just silly things like that. I depended on her way too much, and now I'm lost. There's a part of me that I will never get back from anybody. I never can find somebody like I did with Leslie. She's just irreplaceable. I can't tell you the single thing that I loved most about her. I just know she's a part of me and I was a part of her and she'll continue to live in me every day even though she's not here.

"She had no idea that she touched so many

lives. Everybody I've met through her will come up to me and say, 'You know Leslie was my best friend.' It's just how they felt about her. That's how she made them feel. . . . I don't think I will meet as many people and touch as many lives as she did in her twenty-six years here. I think it takes a longer lifetime than that, and I think her soul was older than what she was, and it was just her time to go."

One could tell how special Leslie was by the massive outpouring of grief after her murder. It was truly remarkable. Those who couldn't attend the funeral took to the Internet, posting their memories on Web sites and blogs. A man identifying himself as Chris H. was transformed back into the boy he was in first and second grade, when Leslie gave him, he said, "my first kiss. Two years to a six- or seven-year-old is a pretty long time, but I felt like I only had a moment before she moved away."

Brian Maucere spoke of meeting Leslie on his first day of college at the University of Georgia, when they were seated next to each other in a statistics class that held three hundred students. "I can't help but wonder how my life would have been different these past eight years if Leslie hadn't turned to me in the middle of class that first day and whispered, 'I think we should be friends.' I'm so glad I said yes, but with Leslie, how could anyone say no?"

A man named Marcus who dated Leslie's roommate in college, said, "She was like the little sister I never had. When I heard the news, I basically felt my heart break."

Leslie's study partner in a medieval literature class in college wrote, "I sat there and cried when I remembered how unbelievably sweet and friendly she was."

Abby Middlebrooks was at the memorial, but she, too, took to the blog designated for memories of Leslie. She said she was impressed by the book of memories sent by workers at the Niebaum-Coppola winery, a book filled with long pages of thoughts to Leslie's family. "And she was only there six months," she marveled.

Abby recalled the sight of Leslie at her wedding in March 2003. "She was beautiful in a red dress and greeted everyone—she passed out programs for me—with her huge, beautiful smile. I am saddened I will never get to return the favor, but I am somewhat at ease knowing Leslie lived life to the fullest always following her heart."

A second remembrance for Leslie was held months later in Ludington, Michigan, at Cathy's congregation. Her friends recalled funny stories about Leslie, and Kelly McCorkle performed a song in sign language called "I Can Only Imagine," which she said "is about going to heaven and seeing Jesus for the first time."

Amy Brown was thinking about Leslie in heaven, too, but it was a bit different from Kelly's scenario. With a twinkle in her eye, Amy said, "I can just see Leslie standing in line, waiting to enter heaven, and God is handing out halos to his angels. She politely declines and says, 'Oh, no, God, I'm here for my tiara.' "

TWENTY-TWO

The $100,000 Reward

On November 12, Napa Mayor Ed Henderson announced that the community had raised $100,000 in reward money for any information leading to the arrest and conviction of whoever was responsible for the double murders on Dorset Street.

"We got pledges anywhere from $500 to $25,000," Henderson said. "It's incredible to think this was done in twenty-four hours. It makes a statement that our community will not tolerate this type of violence and we are appalled this could happen in our community. We are anxious for police to solve this crime. We may fuss at each other, but when it comes to an emergency, we always come together."

A large portion of the money came from the Winegrowers Association, which was eager to catch the killer and keep the reputation of the Napa Valley as sterling as it always had been. The police, meanwhile, were hoping the reward would motivate someone "with critical information" to come forward.

Posters featuring smiling photographs of both women went up all over the Napa Valley and beyond.

At this point, producers from the CBS News program *48 Hours Mystery* were on the case. The planning department never stops scouting for interesting stories that can be turned into prime-time hours, and this one fit the bill, even though there was no suspect and nothing definitive on the horizon. The story of the double murders had been dispersed on the Internet, on television stations in San Francisco, and in an industrywide tip sheet subscribed to by the television networks. The tip sheet, which attempts to be as provocative as possible to draw interest, suggested that the story was about the death of a beauty queen with a Hollywood angle. The "Hollywood angle," of course, was Francis Ford Coppola, who had nothing to do with the story except that one of the dead women happened to work at his winery.

In the New York offices of *48 Hours Mystery,* located in the CBS News broadcast center on West 57th Street, senior story editor Kathleen O'Connell had received the go-ahead on the story from the show's executive producer, Susan Zirinsky. The show's West Coast team was sent to Napa to work the story and line up exclusive interviews. As is often the case, the team did not know where the story was headed but knew that it was of importance. Producer Abra Potkin, well known for her charm and tenacity, and field producer Sue McHugh, a television veteran, flew to San Francisco, while Joanna Cetera, an associate producer based in New York, was assigned to work on the story's East Coast connections in South Carolina and elsewhere. The correspondent, who would come onboard later, was Bill Lagattuta. The team fanned out to talk to friends and family.

At that point, no one had any idea how the story would unfold, and there was a possibility that it would be a story with no ending, meaning no killer would be caught, a possibility that would be disappointing for television but, of course, devastating to the families. The race was on to report and conduct an investigation parallel to the one undertaken by the Napa police.

TWENTY-THREE

Lily

Lily Prudhomme was one of Adriane's newer friends, but they'd grown very close very quickly. They'd met only the year before, but the more they crossed paths, the more both of them realized how much they had in common. Lily, at twenty-five, was a year younger than Adriane, but both worked at the Napa Sanitation District. "She was just one of those outgoing girls in the office," Lily said. "She was an engineer, and then we ended up living across the street from each other."

Adriane eventually moved from that house and into the one on Dorset Street, but for a while, she and Lily discussed moving in together. Lily eventually demurred and instead moved in with her longtime boyfriend, Eric Copple. Still, the relationship between the two women clicked. It seemed as if when you saw one, you saw them both. "It was sort of a fast friendship. We worked together. We saw each other after work. We worked out at the gym together. There were a lot of things," Lily said. "We'd go get our nails done, that kind of girly stuff."

It was one of those friendships earmarked by fun. Adriane and Lily loved Harry Potter books, and when a new one came out, they would rush to buy it and race to read it, calling each other after every chapter. "Adriane had a very easy, endearing quality about her," Lily said. "She was very funny and very smart, very quick-witted. She liked people a lot, and people liked her."

But, Lily is quick to point out, Adriane was no pushover, far from it. "She was very easy to get along with to some extent, but she could also be very difficult. She tended to be a little bossy, and she knew what she wanted. If you ordered food in a restaurant and they didn't bring it correctly, there was no covering it over. You know, there was no 'It's okay, I'll eat it. It's fine.' With Adriane, it was more like 'No, you send this back. This is not what I wanted.' That kind of thing.

"I think a lot of it came from her mother.

I think Arlene probably had some tough times when the kids were young, and she taught all of her girls to be strong and to make their own way and not rely on other people. She told them to get what they needed out of life. She was tough, really funny, but very strong, a strong person emotionally."

Lily was in some ways Adriane's emotional twin; she, too, is strong-willed and engaging and has an outsized personality. With her reddish-brown hair and sassy attitude, she was a good match for Adriane. Theirs was a twenty-hour-a-day relationship, what with work and play, and they discussed every aspect of their lives, including, of course, their boyfriends.

In the summer of 2004, both were having trouble with the men in their lives. Adriane's steady boyfriend was Christian Lee. The relationship was, for the most part, Lily said, fun and even a bit juvenile. She laughed when she thought of what the two did together. "She and Christian played a lot of card games. I think their favorite game was called Spit. And she liked to wrestle. She and Christian used to wrestle all the time. They thought it was great fun."

But the wrestling took place during the good times. There were dark times that Lily heard all about. "When people are dating and you're friends with one of those people, you sort of see their significant others through a filter. Toward the end, I only saw the negative side of Christian, because Adriane would come to work crying, and, of course, being friends, we'd console her, but you start to get to see Christian in this negative light."

Christian's problem, according to what Adriane told Lily and others, was that he would not commit to her, because, he said, a previous girlfriend cheated on him.

Lily could relate. She had her own boyfriend problems with her main squeeze, Eric, a quiet and shy though good-looking guy with wire-rimmed glasses and a goatee who hung out at a local pool parlor without saying much. His defining characteristic was his quiet demeanor, but he was, according to those who know him, very religious. It seemed Lily and Eric had been together forever, but the reality was that they met in high school and had been going out on and off for about eight years. The couple had planned to marry on November 1, 2004, the very day Adriane and Leslie were killed. The wedding was postponed after a spat, and Lily had offered to travel with Adriane to Australia in November 2004. Adriane was happy to have her, and they excitedly made plans.

* * *

Lily and Adriane were part of a group of friends who hung out in Napa, going out to bars like the Bounty Hunter and Downtown Joe's and alternately spending a lot of times at each other's houses. Ben Katz, a musician and Web designer, was in the inner circle. Ben, soft-spoken and witty, likes to wear his hair gelled up in spikes, which, along with slightly bulging eyes, gives him an amusing *Beetlejuice* quality. There was nothing romantic going on between Adriane and him, and there never had been, but Ben was probably Adriane's closest male friend. "I loved Adriane," Ben said. "She was like a sister to me. She was always there, you know, as a friend. Anytime you wanted to talk, anytime you wanted to hang out, she was always there. We would be each other's dates if we didn't have a date for something and had no one else to go with."

Adriane leaned on Ben between relationships and asked him to be her date when she had none. In fact, Adriane asked Ben to accompany her to Lily's wedding in Hawaii. "She was very excited to go, and so was I," he said. "I was, like, 'A ticket to Hawaii? Of course I'll go.' "

Ben met Adriane when they lived next door to each other, although they were never introduced until Ben was actually moving out. They clicked, and, as with Lily, it became a fast friendship. Ben got to know all of Adriane's likes and dislikes, and though he didn't agree with her choices, it didn't really matter. He knew her favorite bands were Nickelback and Maroon 5, bands that Ben didn't especially admire. He knew she liked the television shows *The Real World* and *American Idol* and would sometimes watch them with her even though he thought they were stupid. And then there was Adriane's lackluster cooking. Ben said flatly that Adriane could not cook, but one time she made him a special dish, chicken with Diet Coke. "Well, I ate it," he said, laughing.

Their friendship was bigger than the little things.

"Me and Adriane always confided in each other," he said. "She would always tell me about her boyfriends. She felt free to express herself. She would cry, or she'd be angry, and I would let her. In a way, I was kind of like her protector. If she had a bad night, she'd always come by or give me a call, and we'd just talk and talk until she felt better.

"Six months before she died, my mother died, and I confided in her. She was one of the only people in Napa that I ever really talked to about my mother passing."

It was Adriane who introduced Ben to Leslie when she first hit town. He was sitting at home one night when Adriane called.

"Whatcha doin'?"

"Nothing. I'm kind of tired."

"Why dontcha come down to the Bounty Hunter for a drink?" Adriane asked.

"Nah, I'm beat. I'm gonna turn in early."

"Come on, I have somebody new here you'd probably like to meet."

"I don't think so," Ben said.

"Well, hang on a minute. I'm gonna put her on."

Adriane handed the phone to Leslie.

"Hey there, Ben," she said in her most honey-coated Southern accent. "Why don't you join us down here for a drink?"

Ben perked up. "Who's this?"

"Leslie."

"You sound like you're from the South."

"Good guess, honey. I'm from South Carolina. So, are ya comin'? Adriane really wants you down here."

Ben hesitated; he didn't really want to get dressed up, but he was intrigued. There was something flirtatious in her voice, and suddenly, he wasn't feeling too tired anymore. "I'll be there if you're gonna be there."

"I'll be right here."

Like everyone else, Ben found Leslie to have great charm and, though she was always referred to as a beauty queen since her death, Ben had no idea that was the case. "I just thought she was here to go to law school," he said.

Part of it was Leslie's somewhat chameleonlike looks. In some photos, dolled up for competition, she looks exactly like a beauty queen, but in others, she looks like an attractive woman with a great smile and an open face. Ben liked Leslie from the start, and they had something in common: both had worked at the Niebaum-Coppola winery, though not at the same time. Ben grew up in Southern California but was flown to San Francisco to meet Francis Ford Coppola when he applied for a job doing graphic Web design for the winery. The interview took place at the Zoetrope Studios, and Ben said Coppola sat behind a desk. Behind him was a ghoulish mural from the film *Apocalypse Now,* showing Marlon Brando holding a severed head. "It was a little intimidating, to say the least," Ben said. During the interview, Ben told Coppola he was going to head to Napa afterward, and he knew he had the job when, after the interview was over, Coppola asked Ben if he would drive Coppola and a friend up to Napa. A stunned Ben said yes, and he worked at the winery for two years but left before Leslie got her job.

Ben, Adriane, Lily, Eric, and sometimes Lauren and a few others formed their own small social group and they did a lot of things together or in various combinations. They were having a great time, living the lives of young twenty-something singles in a beautiful location. Their lives were full of fun until Halloween 2004.

The last time Lily saw Adriane was the Friday before Halloween, two days before the murders. Adriane had come to work dressed as a jail bird. "She had a black-and-white-striped uniform on like you'd wear in jail and a little sign around her neck that had a booking number on it," Lily said.

On Monday, Lily wasn't feeling well; she'd been to a party Halloween night and had had another fight with Eric. She was so angry at him that she dropped him off at their apartment and then spent the night at her parents' house; they were out of town in Hawaii. They had bought tickets for that date, thinking Lily and Eric would wed there, and when the wedding was called off, it was too late to get a refund on the plane tickets, so they went anyway.

"I had called in sick to work with a migraine," she said. "And I let people at work know that that's where I was if anybody needed to get hold of me. I woke up around 9:30 to knocking on my parents' door. When I opened it, there were three men standing there with badges wanting to talk.

"They said, 'Did you work with Adriane?' And we have two Adrianes at work, so I clarified, Adriane Insogna? And they said yes, and that she'd been killed the night before. I thought maybe she was hit by a drunk driver. I just assumed it was an accident, but they told me no, it's worse than that. She was murdered."

"The word *murder* was like thunder. I couldn't really see anything after that word," Ben said when he, too, was surprised by a visit from the police.

"You want the world to stop because it's kind of stopped for you," Lily said.

A week after the murder, just before Adriane's funeral, Lily went to Ben with an idea. What if they had a candlelight vigil to remember Adriane and Leslie and speak out against violence?

Lauren Meanza, the sole survivor

Leslie Ann Mazzara, Miss Williamston 2002
(courtesy of Will Tullis)

Adriane
(courtesy of Amanda Vaughan)

ABOVE
Leslie Mazzara
(courtesy of Will Tullis)

RIGHT
Leslie as beauty queen
(courtesy of Will Tullis)

Arlene Allen, Adriane Insogna's mother

Lauren, Arlene, and Rita atop the Sydney Harbor Bay Bridge on November 1, 2004, the day Arlene's daughter Adriane was murdered in Napa (courtesy of Arlene Allen/Bridge Climb)

Adriane and Lily
(courtesy of Arlene Allen)

Adriane and Amanda
(courtesy of Amanda Vaughan)

Adriane, Bridget Domaszek (college friend of both women), and Amanda Vaughan. This was taken in September 2004 and was the last time Amanda saw Adriane. Eventually, police cropped out the other two women and used this photo of Adriane on the flyers looking for information after her death (courtesy of Amanda Vaughan).

Adriane and Carrie Wagner, close college friend
(courtesy of Amanda Vaughan)

Amanda Vaughan, Adriane, and Amanda's husband, Andrew
(courtesy of Amanda Vaughan)

Lauren Meanza, the sole survivor

Leslie Ann Mazzara, Miss Williamston 2002
(courtesy of Will Tullis)

Adriane
(courtesy of Amanda Vaughan)

ABOVE
Leslie Mazzara
(courtesy of Will Tullis)

RIGHT
Leslie as beauty queen
(courtesy of Will Tullis)

Arlene Allen, Adriane Insogna's mother

Lauren, Arlene, and Rita atop the Sydney Harbor Bay Bridge on November 1, 2004, the day Arlene's daughter Adriane was murdered in Napa (courtesy of Arlene Allen/Bridge Climb)

Adriane and Lily
(courtesy of Arlene Allen)

Adriane and Amanda
(courtesy of Amanda Vaughan)

Adriane, Bridget Domaszek (college friend of both women), and Amanda Vaughan. This was taken in September 2004 and was the last time Amanda saw Adriane. Eventually, police cropped out the other two women and used this photo of Adriane on the flyers looking for information after her death (courtesy of Amanda Vaughan).

Adriane and Carrie Wagner, close college friend
(courtesy of Amanda Vaughan)

Amanda Vaughan, Adriane, and Amanda's husband, Andrew
(courtesy of Amanda Vaughan)

Adriane and Josh Reynolds, a friend from Cal Poly and one of the pallbearers at her funeral. His daughter's middle name is Adriane in honor of his friend (courtesy of Amanda Vaughan).

Adriane and unnamed college friend
(courtesy of Amanda Vaughan)

Adriane and Luke, a friend from Cal Poly
(courtesy of Amanda Vaughan)

Adriane and college friends
(courtesy of Amanda Vaughan)

Andrew and Amanda Vaughan with Adriane
(courtesy of Amanda Vaughan)

LEFT
Lily Prudhomme
(CBS News)

RIGHT
Kelly McCorkle
(CBS News)

BELOW
Amy Brown,
Leslie's close
friend
(CBS News)

PJ Clem, Leslie's brother
(CBS News)

Christian Lee, Adriane's boyfriend at the time of her death
(CBS News)

Cathy Harrington, Leslie's mother,
now Reverend Cathy Harrington (CBS News)

Kelly McCorkle, Leslie's close friend and
former Miss South Carolina (CBS News)

Andy Clem, Leslie's brother
(CBS News)

Ben Katz, a close friend of Adriane's
(CBS News)

Eric Copple, Lily's husband, who played a key role
in solving the case (CBS News).

"I was, like, 'That's a great idea. What can I do to help?' " Ben said.

Ben created a flyer that was featured in the newspaper, and before you knew it, they had a vigil planned.

It was set for Sunday, November 14, 2004.

TWENTY-FOUR

"Nothing Is
Going to Be the Same"

That chilly Sunday evening, two weeks after the murders, about a hundred people who knew Adriane and Leslie assembled at Veteran's Memorial Park and held lit candles in honor of the two slain friends. Mayor Ed Henderson was there, along with Lily, Eric, and Ben and some of Adriane's colleagues from the Napa Sanitation District.

Lauren Meanza was in the crowd, although her presence intentionally was kept low-key, and she was guarded by plainclothes Napa police officers. The police detail was with Lauren every time she went to a volleyball game that fall and at various other times when she went out in public. In the days after the slaying, Lauren could not stop thinking of the killer, the man who had nearly run her over coming down the stairs. "I don't understand how a person can do that and go on with his life," she said. "I've thought about that so many times. It's like he is still going on with his life right now without any of this affecting him. Maybe it has affected him, I don't know, but he's still functioning in society after doing something this horrendous. It's incomprehensible to me."

Lily spoke to the crowd, telling them, "We are all grieving, we all hurt, but we are all here together. This crime has taken one of my best friends."

In her quiet moments standing there, Lily's mind went back to some of the great times she and Adriane had together, including one day the previous summer. It was the first day of spring, June 21, and Adriane wanted to celebrate the tenth anniversary of her near-fatal car accident. "She used to call it 'the day I was supposed to die,' " Lily remembered.

Lily, Adriane, Lauren, and an out-of-town friend of Lily's took the day off from work and went to the Great Adventure amusement park. Adriane wasn't morbid about the date or the accident; in fact, whenever she talked about it, she mentioned the people at If Given a Chance, the foundation that helped pay her way through college. "We went on scary rides that day," Lily said. "She was kind of a daredevil, and she and I would go on rides the other two wouldn't go on. It was kind of a 'laugh in the face of danger' day. It was so much fun. We had a great time. It was an Adriane day for sure—she was very present."

Standing nearby at the vigil was Ben Katz. He had his own memories of Adriane at a Halloween party they both attended in 2003. "We went to this big Halloween extravaganza. It was the weekend before Halloween last year, and it was always a lot of fun because we'd both get dressed," he said. "We loved to show off our costumes and have all the 'regular' people look at us. It was cool. I'm always pretty gory for Halloween but Adriane always wore something kind of fun. That year, she had on a poodle skirt, like from the '50s, and her hair was glowing and had, like, fiber optics in it. She was fun, always a lot of fun."

During the vigil, those in the crowd consoled one another, and they listened to the speakers. Some spoke to reporters about what the women had meant to them. Bill Gaffney, who worked at Napa Sanitation District with Adriane and Lily, told the *Napa Valley Register,* "I saw her as a young lady who saw life not as a race but as a journey to be savored every step of the way."

Jim King, founder of the If Given a Chance foundation, praised Adriane for all she had overcome. "Her life was one of giving, one of joy, one of hope," he said. "There is no way that these women brought this upon themselves."

Lily agreed and thought it was likely that someone would come forward, whether because of the $100,000 reward or some other reason. "It seems like somebody must have seen something. Somebody out there knows something, because this kind of thing can't happen. Somebody would have to notice a friend of theirs acting strange or, you know, had bruises or something. It's a violent crime. It doesn't seem like somebody could just walk away from it and be fine.

"I can only imagine that if Adriane knew what was happening, and I assume she did, she would have fought very, very hard. I hope she hurt him."

"Their final thoughts were of pure horror," Ben said. "What Adriane and Leslie had to go through, that to me is more horrifying than death. It's the hardest thing for me to think of."

Lily addressed the crowd one last time, telling them, "This vigil is the last milestone that I looked forward to. Tomorrow is going to be one of the hardest days. When real life hits, then you realize what you're missing, that nothing is going to be the same."

Then she huddled with her boyfriend, Eric, as the crowd began to sing "Amazing Grace."

Ben Katz stood nearby.

"I've gotten pretty angry about what happened, that anybody could do this," Lily said in April 2005. "I'm almost a little afraid to have a face and a name to put the blame on, and all my grief, just hang it on this person. I'm afraid to see who that person might have been. . . . I don't know whether this person is crazy, but it's so out of the realm of the ordinary. It's very hard to wrap my brain around what happened. It just doesn't make any sense, and it's not gonna get any easier because we have a face and a name."

The truth of those words would come back to haunt everyone involved.

TWENTY-FIVE

Was Leslie the Target?

Out of sight from the public, detectives working the case were collecting DNA samples from every male they could locate who was close to Adriane and Leslie. When they got a name, they'd drive out and question the man and ask if he'd voluntarily allow them to take a DNA sample from inside his mouth. Almost all did, but there were a few who refused.

As the investigation progressed, the cops were beginning to form some impressions. They were, of course, still following all leads, but the betting was that the killer likely had targeted Leslie Mazzara. No-nonsense Marsha Dorgan, a police reporter for the *Napa Valley Register*, had heard the same thing. "The most popular theory is most people think that Leslie was the intended victim and that it was probably a disgruntled boyfriend."

Detective Dan Lonegan agreed: "The evidence we have at this point in time shows that most likely Leslie was the target."

There were a couple of reasons for this. First, Leslie—by dint of her engaging personality—attracted men by the bushel. She was new to town and was much more social than her two roommates. She could go nonstop and often did, traveling to San Francisco with her buddies from the winery—the "babe squad"—and dancing the night away. And then there was the winery job itself. At one point, she dealt a lot with the public, and who knew if a guy had fixated on her? It was certainly possible. Because of her magnetism, the police figured that someone had become obsessed with her or she'd inadvertently rejected someone who wanted revenge.

Adriane's mother thought it was likely the killer was after Leslie, and so did Leslie's close friend Amy Brown. "I am convinced of that," she said. "I just think she's a target because she knows more people. She was a little bit more social, and she went out, met millions of new faces, and she ran into old faces from school. I just think she's a target because of who she was."

In contrast to Leslie's, Adriane's life seemed sedate. She'd lived in the Napa Valley her whole life, she was well known, as were her boyfriends, and it seemed you could find out all you needed to know from talking to her mother and a few friends. Her life had ended before it got terribly complicated.

Leslie's life, on the other hand, was a novel, a Southern Gothic, full of intricacies and dark corners, places where a jilted boyfriend or an obsessive admirer might be lurking. Men bought her expensive presents, built shrines to her on the Internet. And someone was sending her cash by mail in unmarked envelopes.

Leslie had told friends about the money and said she didn't know for sure but had an idea who was sending it. That revelation led police to the darkest secret in Leslie's past, a secret so deep that not even Leslie knew about it until she was an adult.

PART TWO

The
Investigation

TWENTY-SIX

A Family Secret

To learn the essential secret of Leslie's life, you have to travel just about as far from Napa as you can in the mainland United States, all the way to the Hardee Correctional Institution in Bowling Green, Florida, a maximum-security prison about one hundred miles east of Tampa. The surrounding area is full of wild birds and vegetation, and Spanish moss hangs from the trees that line the two-lane road that gets you there, State Road 62. Like a lot of interior Florida—far removed from the coastlines and the sedate gated communities of senior citizens—it looks vaguely prehistoric, a place where you easily can imagine dinosaurs roaming. It looks nothing at all like Napa, which is all carefully cultivated beauty. But Hardee County is striking in its own way; here the beauty of nature is wild, untamed. Obviously, the Florida Department of Correction feels the same way about incarcerated men, because the fences around the buildings are festooned with miles and miles of razor ribbon.

And in the middle of all that razor ribbon sits Leslie's biological father, Lenny Mazzara, a father Leslie knew nothing about until she was twenty years old, according to close friend Amy Brown. "The family kind of hid it from her, but she knew of his name and wanted to know where he was and get to know him," Amy said.

Lenny Mazzara now fifty-seven, said friends introduced him to Leslie's mother, Cathy, back in 1976 when they were both living in Orlando. "We just clicked," he said. "It must have been something, because we weren't really physically compatible. She's five-eight, and I'm five-four."

But Lenny does have a certain quiet intensity about him, and he does have piercing blue eyes that no doubt Cathy fell for. And Cathy caught Lenny's eye, too. It's clear he admired her talent and still talks about the way she could cut hair and how "superb" she was at playing classical guitar. You can still hear the surprise in his voice that someone so talented wanted to be with him.

They dated for about a year before they were married, but then things fell apart quickly, according to Lenny. He enjoyed being married to Cathy, at least for a while. "We went to Lamaze classes when she was pregnant, and I was the first one to see Leslie come into the world," he said. "That was really something."

But the stresses of having a child hit the couple hard. Cathy was already raising two children from her first marriage, and Lenny said that, despite what Cathy says about Leslie, her birth sent Cathy into the dark hole of postpartum depression. And they were having big money problems. Cathy lost her income from cutting hair when Leslie was born, and Lenny, by his own admission, was not making much doing odd jobs. Cathy wanted to try counseling, and Lenny went along, but he felt it wasn't getting them anywhere. "When she said something, the counselor would agree with her, and when I said something, he'd agree with me," he said, shrugging his shoulders.

They drifted apart. Cathy stayed in Orlando cutting hair, and Lenny went to Jacksonville, where he managed a music club called the Comic Book. Cathy filed for divorce, and Lenny said the court ordered him to pay Cathy $125 a month in child support. "My lawyer said he could get it lowered, and I said, 'Lowered? Do you know how much it costs to raise a kid?' "

He told his lawyer to leave it alone. He and Cathy stayed friendly enough—Lenny is still close to Cathy's mother, Judy—and he attended Leslie's first birthday party. But then Lenny had problems of his own, big problems.

The story of why Lenny Mazzara is incarcerated is a shocking, violent, and convoluted tale involving drugs, rock and roll, and murder. Back in 1980—two years after Leslie was born and two years after Cathy divorced him—Lenny became the manager for the Rocco Marshall Band in Florida, but his secondary job, according to court records, was that of a drug dealer and small-time hood. According to the Florida State Attorney's office, Lenny's boss, James Provost, a local gangster, was owed $10,000 in drug money by the wife of George "Rocco" Marshall. Provost told Marshall, according to court records, that he would forgive the debt if Marshall found someone to kill a man named Frank Ilhenfeld, who supposedly also owed Provost even more money. Two men, Barry Hoffman and Frank White, were enlisted to commit the murder, which, court papers say, was ordered by Lenny working for Provost. Hoffman was to get $5,000 and White $500.

Court records and newspaper articles from the time tell the story.

On September 21, 1980, Hoffman and White went to a seedy Ramada Inn in Jacksonville to carry out the contract on Ilhenfeld. They surprised him and began stabbing him, when, unfortunately for all concerned, Ilhenfeld's girlfriend, Linda Sue Parrish, picked that moment to enter the room. The two men pounced on Parrish, records state, and she was stabbed to death and had her neck slit, along with that of her boyfriend. It was a horrific small-town gangland murder and made headlines in Jacksonville. Eventually, Marshall was given immunity, but the rest of the principals were indicted. Provost died of heart failure before trial. Hoffman, White, and Lenny Mazzara were convicted of the murders (a new trial was ordered for Hoffman in 2001, but he remains in prison). Lenny was sentenced to two consecutive life terms and received an additional thirty-year sentence for conspiracy. He insists to this day that he is innocent, even after serving twenty-six years in prison. He says he's become something of a jailhouse lawyer and is hopeful of getting his conviction overturned.

On a visit to Hardee, it's hard to see that small-time hood when you meet Lenny today.

He seems more like someone's handyman than someone's "muscle," like a guy you'd meet on a construction site on Long Island, which is where he's from.

Lenny says that, whatever the trouble between Cathy and him, he was always close to Grammy, Cathy's mother and Leslie's grandmother. Grammy must have had a soft spot for "Husband Number 2," as he calls himself, because she continued to send him photographs of Leslie growing up, even when he was incarcerated. He has the photographs until she was six years old, but then he figures Cathy must have put her foot down, because he was cut off completely. Over the years, he told other inmates about his only child, Leslie, and they asked why he didn't do more to get in touch with her. "I told them, when she's eighteen, if she wants to find me, she can," he said.

Leslie did not find Lenny when she was eighteen. It took two years longer. Grammy had insisted to Cathy that she tell Leslie about her father. Cathy relented. One day, Lenny got a letter. "[Leslie] wrote that her mother told her where I was, and she told me she was not happy with her mother for hiding me all those years," Lenny said. "She sent me a bunch of photos of herself."

Overwhelmed by all the years he'd missed, Lenny had someone send Leslie $150, but he insisted that's all the money he ever sent her. He also picked up the phone and called her. "She was excited, and I told her I'd call her again, like maybe once a month, and she said, 'You can call every day,' but I told her it was like $20 for a phone call, and she said, 'Okay, maybe once a month is fine, then,' " he said, laughing.

Then, one day, Leslie came to see her father accompanied by Grammy. "Grammy—she's a great woman," Lenny said. "She could find good in the devil. She was Leslie's best friend."

Father and daughter sat on either side of a prison picnic table and stared at each other. "I saw her mother in her, and she saw me in her," he said.

"Every child wants to know, 'Do I look like this person?' " said Amy. "They just talked about life, and she found out why she looks the way she looks [Leslie was dark-haired, while her brothers, with a different father, have reddish hair like their mother's] and why she's short. He knew about Leslie's life and where she was and had pictures of her. It just gave her a little closure to find her father and discuss life with him. She enjoyed that."

Leslie wound up visiting Lenny four or five

times, once or twice driven by a current boyfriend who waited hours for her outside in the parking lot. Lenny would end up learning a lot about Leslie's boyfriends in their talks. She told him she wanted to get married, but not, she said, like her mother, who'd been married multiple times. "She wanted to do it once and get it right," Lenny said.

Letters went back and forth, and Leslie made sure to give her father some current photographs of herself. Lenny said Leslie wasn't much good at writing. "One time, she sent me two back-to-back and said, 'Dad, I know you're gonna have a heart attack, but I had time to write . . .' "

After Leslie won the Miss Williamston contest, he said, "She came running down here, and boy was she excited. She had on a little bracelet, and she was just so happy."

Leslie told him a story about how her friend Kelly McCorkle had lent her a "smoking" dress for the competition which showed off all her assets. After Leslie won and found out she'd be competing against Kelly for the Miss South Carolina crown, Kelly was blunt: "Okay, this time, you're not getting that dress."

The last time Lenny heard from Leslie personally was when she moved to California, but Grammy kept writing to let him know how she was doing. And then came the day when he was called into the chaplain's office, never a good sign in prison. The chaplain, whom Lenny considered a hypocrite, said he'd received a phone call from Grammy. He told Lenny the news and asked if he'd like to pray, but Lenny said he wanted to get back to his detail, where he felt more comfortable talking to friends about what had happened.

"It screwed me up real bad," he said by way of understatement. One can only imagine the powerlessness and despair he must have felt. He waited twenty years for his only child to contact him, and when she did, she was a breath of fresh air, and then, suddenly, she was out of his life forever. Lenny was not allowed to go to her funeral and had only Grammy's letters and his jailhouse buddies to console him. The word *lockup* probably never had felt so definitive.

In his grief, Lenny wrote to the Napa police, asking them for information about his daughter. He never heard from them, he said, until one day Detective Shulman and Sergeant Tom Piper showed up at Hardee. It was inevitable, really, given the nature of the crime Lenny was convicted of. There aren't too many contract hits carried out by stabbing, and the police understandably were curious about whether there was any way Leslie's death was connected to her father's crime.

They wanted to know if Lenny had any enemies, if maybe someone from his past was seeking revenge. "I thought that was stupid," he said. "It was twenty-six years ago."

What about other inmates or even officers who might be out to get him? That made Lenny think. He'd had a few run-ins over the years, but he couldn't come up with anyone who might do something like that.

"Were you sending her money?" they asked out of the blue.

He explained that he had at one time, but that was all.

"Well, someone was sending her money," one of the cops said.

"How much money?" Lenny asked.

"A lot."

Lenny was curious. "What's a lot?"

They wouldn't say.

Was the money connected to Leslie's and Adriane's deaths? The cops made it clear that they were not there to answer questions. They were through with Lenny.

TWENTY-SEVEN

"As Long as I'm Alive . . ."

Arlene Allen said she'd always loved puzzles and often curled up on the couch in her tiny, 500-square-foot apartment to work on the daily crossword. "I have always been interested in crossword puzzles, word games, and the like, but now, since Adriane's death, it's become kind of an obsession with me, in that when I'm by myself at home, I can settle and focus on a crossword puzzle, and all my other thoughts just disappear," she said. "It's kind of like my little magic place that I go to get away, and it's been very helpful, almost an obsession with me these days."

In the weeks and then months after her daughter's murder, Arlene, who suffered from depression before the murder, did anything she could to keep her mind working but not *thinking*. She began playing mah-jongg with her friend Lauren and a group of women in nearby Santa Rosa to stay occupied. "It's a wonderful game, and I can focus and not think any thoughts that would lead me down sad paths. It's been a wonderful addition to my life," she said.

The group of women Arlene played with did their best to talk about anything other than what was foremost on their minds: Adriane's murder and the quiet police investigation. They were all wondering what was happening and would have loved to ask Arlene but did not out of respect. For her part, Arlene learned and played the game with gusto, concentrating on the little tiles click-clacking in front of her and putting her living nightmare aside.

"She's got this huge hole in her life, in her heart," says Lauren. "She puts on a really good public face, but when she's at home, she'll collapse in the shower and cry like everybody else will. She has a hard time getting up some mornings. It's hard for her, because they were buds as well as mother and daughter."

What Arlene was not able to do was to keep working as the office manager for a local CPA firm. "The horrendous weight of Adriane's murder just made it impossible for me to worry about other people," Arlene said. "I realized then that I needed to focus on myself and whatever it would take to get me through this really difficult time. Adriane would not want me to lie down and die with grief over her death. She really lived life to the fullest, she was so adventurous, so full of life."

In retrospect, she recalled the "euphoric feeling" she had when she was atop the Sydney Harbor Bridge and said she now believes it was Adriane's "spirit sailing over me. I really do believe that she was there and experiencing the joy of that with me." Because of that feeling and because her own trip to Australia was cut short, Arlene resolved that she was going to return and climb the bridge once again, perhaps on the anniversary of Adriane's death.

Arlene, who understandably has a deep sadness about her blue eyes, made a number of hard decisions after Adriane's death. For one thing, she decided there was no way she was going to leave Calistoga. "I can understand how people think, well, there's all these painful memories here, but they're not painful to me," she said. "When I'm in town, I see places that remind me of Adriane, and it's comforting. I know what a happy life she had here, and when I see the places that remind me of her, like Checkers, where she worked from the time she was sixteen and on, it feels good.

"As long as there are people here who loved Adriane, her memory is alive."

There are times, though, Arlene confided, when she feels pulled down by the heavy emotional weight of being the mother of the dead woman. It is sometimes an anchor threatening to deepen her depression. There is such an outpouring from the community, so many people who want to hug and comfort her, that at times she admitted to finding it "a bit difficult." When that happens, when "I think I'm not up for it," she travels to nearby Santa Rosa, "where I can be anonymous and go about my business without having to focus on it."

Another decision Arlene made was to keep her daughter's car, a 2004 Toyota 4Runner. Adriane considered it her baptism into adulthood, a car that symbolized that she was a professional woman, an engineer. "She researched buying a car for years, and she wanted an SUV and settled on this Toyota; she bought it in July 2004, so she only had it a few months. She loved this car, and the day after she bought it, she sent me an e-mail with a picture of her 'new baby.' We used to go to San Francisco to see baseball games, and she always wanted to take her new car, even though it would have been faster to take the two-seater Geo. I keep the car because it reminds me of her, and it's the same reason I keep the buttons on the radio stations set to the stations she used to listen to. Now I listen to them, and I feel closer to her. I feel she's with me."

It is tactile memory Arlene is after, a sense she can pull her daughter a tiny bit closer by reaching out and touching the buttons she once touched, putting her fingers where Adriane's once were. Arlene's musical tastes have evolved, she joked, from oldies to rock and alternative. She listens a lot to Alice 97.3, one of Adriane's favorite stations. The car is very much still Adriane's: it has the Cal Poly bumper sticker on it that Adriane put there. As she drives, Arlene not only listens to the radio stations her daughter listened to, but she also plays the last CD Adriane bought. It was Maroon 5, and Adriane played it over and over, especially her favorite song, "She Will Be Loved."

"As long as I'm alive, Adriane will be loved," she said, a tear falling down her cheek.

It's not the only thing Arlene does to continue to feel Adriane's spirit. All of her mail is forwarded to her mother, even some of the bulk mail like Adriane's Victoria's Secret catalogs. Arlene doesn't have much space, but she finds herself keeping those catalogs and other junk mail sent to Adriane. "Part of me wants to keep Adriane alive and not deal with desolation," she said.

In the months after the tragedy, Arlene spent a lot of time and still does with her friend Lauren, who was in Australia with her when she received news of Adriane's death. Lauren is a bright spot in Arlene's life, always there literally to lend a shoulder to cry on.

What bothers Arlene most, she admitted sadly, is the reaction of her other two daughters, who are having a hard time dealing with their sister's death. According to Arlene, they do not want to discuss it, not even with her. In a powerful statement, Arlene admitted she feels disconnected from her daughters in a frightening way. "I feel as though we've all stepped on a land mine, and we're flying up in the air and lost our limbs, and we can't reach out and hold each other. It's terrible," she said as the tears welled up.

Those are her bad moments, but there are plenty of moments when she feels at peace with herself. She goes through her day with her faithful friend Lauren. The two work out at Curves, an exercise facility designed exclusively for women. Afterward, they sometimes skinny-dip in Lauren's hot tub, and other times, they stop at Checkers to have lunch, where, invariably, they run into owner Ron Golden, who said he can't forget Adriane's smiling face.

"The biggest thing I have to get used to is the loss of Adriane, and that's going to take the rest of my life," Arlene said.

TWENTY-EIGHT

The Men in Her Life

Little by little, the men who were close to Adriane Insogna were crossed off the list of suspects as their DNA did not match the sample of blood found at the crime scene. The detective work was going as planned, but it wasn't really moving ahead. The cops checked on the criminal pasts of everyone in the neighborhood, and while a few had rap sheets, all had alibis or DNA that did not match the blood found in the house. People were being eliminated from the list, but the cops were no closer to finding the killer.

Then, out of nowhere, they heard about the suicide of a young male restaurant worker. The buzz in town was that he may have had something to do with the murders and had killed himself out of guilt.

The word on the street was that the young busboy had been given a ride the night of the murder by a friend who found him bloodied and scratched. Christian Lee, who worked in the bars and restaurants of Napa, heard the story and immediately reported it to the cops, but they assured him they'd gotten there first and checked it out. They even had secured DNA from the busboy's remains.

It came back negative. In death, the busboy was cleared, as the mystery continued.

As they investigated Leslie's life, Napa detectives thought it made the most sense to start with her current boyfriends—the men she was dating around the time of her murder—before casting a wider net. To learn more about Leslie's life, investigators were checking her cell-phone records, interviewing friends at the winery, and talking to Lauren Meanza about the social lives of the dead women in the weeks leading up to the murders.

And then they got a phone call that saved them a lot of time and trouble. It was from a young woman named Vanessa Schnurr, who lives in Atlanta. She told the cops that she'd gone to the University of Georgia with Leslie and, even more pertinent, that Vanessa and another college friend, Katie Norris, had visited Leslie in Napa just three weeks before the murders. In fact, Vanessa said, she and Katie had slept in Leslie's room, in the very bed where she was later attacked by the intruder.

"That place is still very vivid in my mind," Vanessa said. "The sounds, the smells . . . it's just been very haunting to us. We walk through that house over and over in our minds. It was extremely small, like a bungalow from the '30s, and still had the original hardwood floors. You could hear everything through every door."

Katie agreed: "It was kind of easier for me, because we had been to the house, and when I found out the news, I could see myself walking back through there and going upstairs to the bedroom where we stayed. The top two steps were creaky."

Vanessa remembered that the first night they got in—October 7—they arrived at the house on Dorset Street after midnight, and, try as they might to be quiet, "those top steps creaked so much that we woke Adriane up. She came out and said hey and then went back to sleep."

Detectives asked the women to tell them

about life in the house, what the roommates were like when they were together, and how they got along. Vanessa and Katie said they did not notice any overt tension among the women. They had no doubt Leslie was very happy, but it was more because of the life she was building in Napa than because of her roommates. They all got along and interacted well in the house, but "they were a bit more reserved" than Leslie, Vanessa said. "Over the course of our stay, Leslie mentioned that Lauren and Adriane didn't really understand her, the way she was a social butterfly."

Vanessa recalled a comment Leslie made that indicated she and her roommates were not on the same wavelength. "Leslie said, 'I'm so glad to have y'all here because y'all just understand and y'all are happy for me that I'm happy.' "

At one point, one of the roommates—Vanessa can't remember which one—asked Leslie, "How do you get all these dates?" And Leslie answered, "Well, you can't just sit at home. You have to go out and meet people."

Leslie told Vanessa and Katie that she was exasperated at times with Adriane and Lauren. "It's like they expect men to come on by and knock on their door," she said.

The cops told Katie and Vanessa that they'd heard Leslie dated "a lot" of men, and indeed, that was the perception running rampant through the Napa community. The *48 Hours* producers working on the story heard it often, and whenever it was said, whoever said it, it was said in a way that indicated the speaker meant something more by it, as though there were something wrong with the way Leslie operated. Katie and Vanessa wanted to shut that perception down; it wasn't fair, and it just wasn't the way Leslie really was, they said.

"Leslie was simply going out with people. She had a large circle of friends," Vanessa said. "Leslie was very electric. Whenever Leslie walked into the room, everybody stopped and looked. She had an ability to draw you to her. It was just amazing. She had the ability to make anyone feel comfortable in any situation. She had this look that would make anyone feel comfortable, and I think with men, that look could be misconstrued as 'Oh, that's the look. She's giving me the look.' But it wasn't like that. Leslie was just a social butterfly. Sitting at home was not Leslie's style.

"I don't think she was that serious about any man in her life. She had even made a comment to me that she wasn't finished being Leslie. She wasn't ready to be Leslie and whoever forever."

And if men went a bit overboard with Leslie, well, that wasn't her fault. Vanessa and Katie had seen it all back in Georgia, the extravagant things men would do to try to win Leslie's favor. "Men always wanted to make Leslie happy," Vanessa said, "and if they thought they could buy her flowers, or buy her jewelry, or even help her out by buying her a car, they would do it just because to see Leslie happy made them happy, I think. I don't think it was because they expected to buy Leslie, because she just wasn't that type, but guys were constantly showering her with gifts."

Life in Napa was no different. When Leslie first picked up her friends at the San Francisco airport, she told them that she had a new man in her life named Beau. She was sorry they would not get to meet him on their trip, because he was on a business trip, but they'd spent the previous day together. Beau had even made Leslie a personalized CD, and they listened to it the whole time they were in Leslie's car. "She was really excited about it," Vanessa said.

The next day, Leslie took them to the Niebaum-Coppola winery so they could have a tour and see where she worked. Sure enough, there were two dozen roses waiting in her office for her. "It was so big, and she was so excited," Katie said. "She said, 'Come here, guys, you've gotta see this. You've gotta see this.' And she said, 'They were sent by Beau. He's so dreamy.' And we read the card, and, you know, of course, being girls, we oohed and ahhed."

So Beau seemed cool, but they never met him. However, the women told detectives, they did meet Leslie's other main squeeze, a guy named John DeMarco, who was about thirty-five years old, and he was someone they thought the cops should be looking at. DeMarco was tall and good-looking and tried to pass himself off as wealthy, but Katie and Vanessa had their doubts. They were suspicious of him, and after hearing of Leslie's murder, they had fixated on him of all the people they'd met in Napa. Leslie had been dating him for a while and had even arranged for DeMarco to take her friends around to wineries while she was at work. But the day started off poorly when DeMarco spotted the flowers sent by Beau. He was not happy.

As Katie saw it, she thought DeMarco became uncomfortable right away. "I'm a very intuitive person," she said, "and it's just that vibe you get from someone. I'll never forget his eyes, ever! They were dark. He had this very dark evil around him."

"I think Leslie was starting to have some doubts about his sincerity," Katie said.

Vanessa agreed. "He was like the slickest car salesman you'd ever wanna meet. He was a smooth talker, and I think Leslie wanted to know if he was genuine or a salesman."

The women did not like the energy he was throwing off, especially after one incident they witnessed in a bar when they were out with DeMarco and Leslie.

"Leslie was approached by a friend," Katie said, "solely as a friend. It was a casual acquaintance, just some guy she worked with, and John became eerily uneasy, and it was obvious that he was not comfortable with her talking to another man. It was strange, because before, there was this very fun atmosphere, but he was insecure that she was speaking to another man, and there was this dark cloud around him. It was very eerie, like I said."

The best time the three friends had that weekend was on Saturday afternoon, when they drove to the Bus Stop Café in San Francisco, where alumni from the University of Georgia gathered to watch their beloved Bulldogs take on the Volunteers from the University of Tennessee. The Bulldogs won, and when they got back to Dorset Street, the three friends were so tired they just had pizza at the house and gabbed all night. "It was such a quiet house, and I remember thinking it was a little like Mayberry," Vanessa said. "I live in Atlanta, so we'd never do what we did there. We slept with the bedroom window wide open, and the back door was open three or four inches so Adriane's cat could come and go. I never thought anything bad could happen there."

While talking to detectives, the women went back over all the photographs they'd taken the day DeMarco escorted them around to the wineries. That's when all their feelings about him were cemented. "We probably took a good two rolls of film," Katie said. "And he's not in a single picture that we have. He either insisted on taking the picture, or if the staff at the wineries were taking the picture, he would just make sure he was not in them, even though he might have been sitting right next to one of us at the tasting tables. It's very odd."

About a week before she was murdered, Leslie told Vanessa as well as Amy Brown that she'd gotten a "creepy" e-mail from DeMarco. It came after Leslie sent DeMarco an e-mail saying she wanted to date other people and considered their relationship nonexclusive. DeMarco answered immediately with an e-mail Leslie thought inappropriate. She called Amy and said, "What do you think about this e-mail? I'm going to read it to you, and tell me what you think."

Vanessa heard about the e-mail, too, and said, "It was, like, 'I can't believe you're doing this to us.' It came across like he was a very possessive man. It was definitely worrisome."

"It's hard to remember every word now," Amy said, "but it came across as arrogant and a little ballsy. I feel that if he felt betrayed, there's definitely a motive there, if he lost something that he thought he had. He could get angry."

The detectives began to look a bit more closely at DeMarco, and nearly immediately they discovered the reason for his edginess and why he was not in any of those photos: he had a longtime girlfriend. He wasn't quite married, but he had been in a committed thirteen-year relationship with another woman, his live-in girlfriend. They decided to keep an eye on DeMarco and got his DNA.

When *48 Hours* producers contacted him to talk about Leslie, he denied even knowing her.

TWENTY-NINE

Donald the Firefighter

Katie and Vanessa may not have been aware of him, but there was another man in Leslie's life, a tall, good-looking firefighter type named Donald McGowan, who had met Leslie just before she moved in with Lauren and Adriane. One woman who met him and found out that he had casually dated Leslie said it was proof positive for her, at least, that Leslie had a way of charming men that few women possess. "He's ruggedly handsome and the kind of guy every woman wants," she said.

Donald met Leslie when they were both at a bar called Riverside. "We locked eyes and started mingling," he said. "It was as simple as that."

They started talking, and it turned out that

Leslie lived right around the corner from him. "We were friends," he said.

But she really caught his eye a couple of days later when he saw her jogging around his neighborhood "in these little shorts." He was hooked, and they began not really dating but hanging out with each other. "It wasn't real serious, and it was not a full relationship," he said. "I don't think either of us wanted that, anyway. She was just over here having a good time, and I understood."

Leslie was extremely attracted to Donald's earthiness and sexuality, and as it developed, he said she would sometimes call him late in the evening and they occasionally comforted each other late at night. It went on for a while, but eventually, they stopped doing what they were doing because each wanted to pursue other relationships. For whatever reason, despite their attraction, neither took the other that seriously.

"She called me about three weeks before the murder, and we talked for about five or ten minutes," Donald said. "I told her I was with somebody full-time now, and she told me she was dating a couple of guys. She sounded good, I thought."

Napa cops tracked Donald down through Leslie's cell phone, and he willingly agreed to give them a DNA sample.

THIRTY

Return to Dorset Street

On December 30, 2004, Adriane Insogna would have turned twenty-seven years old. Two months had passed since her murder, and there was very little news to report. It was the saddest of days for Adriane's family, because the killer had not been caught, and there was the sinking realization that the tragedy had begun to fade for some people. Napa residents would never completely forget, but the murders weren't always on their minds as they were when they first happened. But for Adriane and Leslie's families, frustration was building. At that point, they knew few of the details, and, while they had faith in the police, it was hard *not knowing*.

Without solid facts, all anyone had were theories. At the offices of the *Napa Valley Sentinel*, publisher Harry Martin, who wears two hats as a dyed-in-the-wool newspaperman and senior member of the city council, surmised that the killer had been an immigrant laborer long gone to Mexico. "It's a very common thing," Martin said. "We had another murder up here at a veteran's home, and they fled to Mexico. A lot of these people flee to Mexico. Someone without a green card, an illegal alien, and we have a lot of them around."

Some people bought into that, while others were simply tired of speculating. They just wanted answers. Young women were especially anxious and took special precautions when they went out alone or when they were walking to their cars at night. A lot of the restaurants and stores in the Napa Valley were staffed with young women, and they never forgot for one moment the double murders on Halloween. They would not let their guard down until the police found the killer. "It's even worse if it was random," one said. "I want them to tell me who did it and how he was connected to those two girls."

The waiting was hard on both families but in different ways. Living in the Napa Valley, Adriane's family faced a constant barrage of questions from neighbors. The neighbors were concerned, but the questioning grew painful, and the family sometimes wished they lived farther away. Meanwhile, Leslie's family, having returned to their homes in Michigan and South Carolina, felt out of touch and wished they lived closer.

Some of the only solid information came from friends who had been allowed into the Dorset Street house to remove the dead women's possessions. Adriane's friend Derek Santiago was one of only three people allowed inside. He was met at the door by a police chaplain, who led the way. It was hard, not knowing if he should look or where he should look. There were no instructions for this kind of thing. He had no idea what he would see and was very anxious.

"What caught me by surprise was just how normal everything was, to a degree," Derek said.

The kitchen looked exactly as it did that Halloween night. An open bottle of sherry was near the stovetop, obviously having been used for cooking. There were notes on the refrigerator about volleyball games and necessities to pick up for Adriane's Australia trip. Derek had the sense that Adriane could walk into the kitchen at any moment, or perhaps he'd hear her coming down the stairs. What was different—very different—about the house was the quiet. It was eerie.

Derek moved to the staircase to head up to Adriane's bedroom, where he saw the first evidence that not all was right. A piece of the wallboard along the stairs was missing, as was a piece of carpet. No one was saying anything; they were all moving quietly, reverentially, almost as though they didn't want to disturb what was now sacred ground. They all knew that by heading upstairs, they were about to witness the scene of the crime, and they cringed inwardly.

"I walked upstairs, and what really struck home the most is what we didn't see, what you didn't have to see," Derek said. "You could almost feel it by looking. The scene had been cleaned."

Where they expected blood, there was none, and that in itself was disquieting. The house had been picked apart, first by investigators, then by forensics people, and finally by the cleaners who had come along to wipe away the sights and smells of death. Someone had done a very thorough job of cleaning, so thorough that the varnish was missing from the floor. Derek hesitantly walked into Adriane's room, stopping for a moment at the door to make sure he was up to the task. Taking even one step was very hard.

"For me, it was so difficult knowing that I

was standing in the spot where my friend had died," he said. "The missing varnish made it very easy to get a visual idea of what happened, how it could have happened, not that I know anything more than anybody else, but I've got a pretty good idea."

Derek collected Adriane's belongings and got out of the house as soon as he could.

He didn't know about anyone else, but to him, it was haunted.

THIRTY-ONE

The Youngbloods

Because Leslie had lived in Napa for only about six months, most of her contacts and ex-boyfriends were back east so that was the next logical stop for Napa detectives. There were fertile leads back in South Carolina, Georgia, and Tennessee that needed to be checked out. Leslie's close friend Amy, who had spoken to her every day, was high on the list of those to interview, largely because she knew so much about Leslie's personal life. But even Amy did not know everything about Leslie. Asked by a detective if she could make a list of everyone Leslie knew, especially men, Amy said, "I can't do it. I don't think I will meet as many people and touch as many lives as she did in her twenty-six years here."

But the detective who questioned her made it easier. He zeroed in on one person in particular and warned Amy, "I'm going to tell you something, and I want you to tell me how it makes you feel."

"Okay."

She girded herself for the worst, for another horrid detail about the unspeakable crime that had robbed her of her life's richest relationship.

"Do you know Lee Youngblood Sr.?" the detective asked.

Lee Senior was the father of Lee Junior, who had lived with Leslie just before she'd gone west; the cops were following up on the persistent rumor that Leslie had fled the relationship, that there was something about the relationship they ought to know.

It was not the question she'd been expecting. She was a little bewildered.

"I've met him a couple of times," Amy said.

"How do you feel about him? What's your general impression?"

Amy didn't hold back. "He gives me the creeps a little bit, to be honest about it."

She knew that Lee Senior seemed almost more bent out of shape about the breakup between his son and Leslie than his son had been, and she also knew that Lee Senior called Leslie so often that there were times she would not answer her phone.

The detective wrote something down. "Well, if I told you that Lee Senior called Leslie twice on Halloween night, how would that make you feel?"

Amy felt chill bumps on her arms, and her hair stood on edge. "I don't like that at all. At all," she repeated. "There's no reason for the father to be calling her. I don't know too many dads who would do that. I've never had an ex-boyfriend's father call me. I think it's very weird."

Thinking about that conversation later, Amy said, "I don't know if he had anything to do with this crime but he makes me very uneasy."

Lee Youngblood Jr., then twenty-seven, first became aware of Leslie back in 2003, when he was judging at a beauty contest in South Carolina. Interestingly, it was not the pageant in which Leslie competed—she was merely there to support her best bud, Kelly McCorkle. Lee was a man about town in and around Columbia, Georgia, where he lived, with the raffish good looks of Matthew McConaughey and a pronounced Southern twang. His father is a prominent lawyer and well-to-do, so Lee is a catch and he knows it. Outfitted with a Rolex he brandishes to great effect, Lee admitted to being a player with the ladies—until, that is, he met Leslie. "When I met her, I didn't know what hit me," he said.

Unlike a lot of Leslie's other admirers, Lee did not spy her across a crowded room or lock eyes with her in a bar. He didn't even notice her at first; he only met her because a friend of his rushed up at one point during the beauty pageant and said, "There's a girl here you just have to meet."

Soon enough, the friend introduced him to Leslie, and Lee asked to borrow a pen. Leslie was coquettish and agreed to lend him the pen only if she'd get it back with his phone number. "We began flirting with each other, and by the end of the night I had asked for her phone number," he said. "That first phone call went great. We had a million things to talk about, and we talked for hours."

But when he asked Leslie for a date, she said no—she was too busy. Lee wasn't used to that, and he dissected her reluctance over and over with friends until they were sick of hearing about it. Most women jumped at the chance to go out with him, so he was surprised but also increasingly interested in this Southern belle who had turned him down. He kept calling, and she kept saying no. Soon enough, the phone calls were falling off, and Lee decided to do something dramatic—he sent Leslie pink roses.

It worked. Leslie said yes. They went on a date and soon they were going out hot and heavy. They'd become, he said, "an item."

Amy agreed that, yes, Leslie was head over heels in love with Lee and she considered it mutual. She was happy for her friend. "I believe that Lee loved Leslie with all his heart," she said. "This relationship was solid, real solid. She would always say to me, 'You know, I think this is the guy that I'm going to marry.' She felt that way about Lee. I felt that Lee and she were going to be married."

It certainly seemed that way. Lee was going all out. It turned out he had a romantic streak in him a mile wide. When he was wooing Leslie, he decided they needed a "special date." At that point, Leslie was still in school in Athens, Georgia, and Lee was living in South Carolina. He drove down and rented a room, but before picking up Leslie, he filled the room with candles, champagne, and pink roses, together with petals on the floor that led from the front door to the bed. One might think that would be enough for any woman, but Lee wasn't done. After Leslie was bowled over, he then handed her a letter professing his eternal love and then, for the topper, he produced one single pink rose that he'd had dipped in 24-carat gold. Even Leslie, well known for her loquacity, was speechless. She was his—for a time.

After graduating from the University of Georgia, Leslie moved in with Lee and not only were they happy but Lee's entire family was happy. Lee's father met Leslie and couldn't have been more pleased. "She was just a joy to be around," Lee Senior said. "We'd do anything in the world for her."

His son had made a great match. Lee's family let Lee and Leslie live in his grandmother's house rent free and, in January, 2004, Leslie went on a cruise with the whole Youngblood family. The cruise—which sailed out of Charleston to Cozumel, Mexico, the Grand Cayman Islands, and Key West, Florida—came at a key point in the relationship. Leslie had told her father, Lenny, that she expected Lee might propose while at sea and, if he didn't, "she was out of there." The thing is, Lee *did* intend to propose. Lee Senior said he even helped his son pick out the ring but Lee Junior never brought it on the cruise, and Lee Senior said he has no idea why. "I didn't try to control anything pertaining to them," he said. "This was my son's thing. Whatever made him happy was fine with me."

During the cruise, Leslie later told Amy, she began seeing a side of Lee's family—specifically his father—that she didn't like. "Lee's dad made her feel very uncomfortable," Amy said. "He began calling Leslie all the time. She wouldn't answer the phone at the house but he owned the house that they lived in and sometimes he would come over unannounced. So it made her feel unnerved and she knew that if she made a decision to go any further in a relationship with the son that, one day, she would also be in this family."

Lee Senior denies calling Leslie over and over. But for some reason, soon after the cruise and after only a couple of months living together, Leslie told Lee that she was breaking it off and needed time to find herself. This occurred in the spring of 2004, just before Leslie decided to go spend time with her mother in California.

"I'd have to say that Lee was a little bit more heartbroken than Leslie," Amy said.

Even when she was living in Napa, Leslie did talk to Lee Junior from time to time. Leslie thought that, because of the abrupt breakup and the way she left town, that perhaps she ought to write some type of explanatory letter to Lee Senior, Amy said. She theorizes that, if Lee Senior was behind Leslie's murder, perhaps it had something to do with betrayal. "I think the father was thinking, for sure, that this woman is going to be his son's wife," Amy said. "Maybe he was upset with Leslie."

Lee Senior said he was not upset by the breakup so much as surprised by the abruptness of it. "I didn't pry into it that much," he said. "It surprised me that she left without saying goodbye to Elizabeth and myself." Lee Senior said he and his wife had no idea Leslie and his son had even broken up until "Elizabeth just happened to go by [the house Leslie was sharing with Lee Junior] on her way back from Augusta and everything was cleared out of Leslie's bedroom. My son didn't say what happened and we didn't inquire."

No one thinks that Lee Junior had anything to do with Leslie's murder. He was told about Leslie's death by the same buddy who had introduced them to each other back at the beauty pageant. The buddy called Lee the day after Halloween, told him he had some news and that he should just stay put. He then drove two hours to deliver the news in person. Lee was beside himself with grief and slept on his living-room floor that night with a baseball bat, imagining he could kill the guy who had killed Leslie. His friend stayed with him the whole night.

After the murders, Lee Senior, a lawyer, reached out to the Napa police. He may have realized the police would come knocking once they checked Leslie's phone records and saw that he had called twice on Halloween. Rather than wait for their suspicions to fester, Lee Senior took the offensive. He called the police and tried to explain the two phone messages he'd left for Leslie on Halloween. "She had been looking for her birth certificate, and I searched my house and office, and they had not turned up," he said. "It was coincidental. It just happened to be the day she was killed."

But even months later, it was clear the Napa police had questions about Lee Senior. "I think he was infatuated with her," Jeff Troendly said in the summer of 2006. "More so than his son. We never heard from Lee Junior, only Dad."

When asked about this, Lee Senior said, "I was not infatuated with her, no sir. The last thing I would do is get infatuated with Lee's girlfriend. I have a thirty-five-year marriage going on. I don't want to monkey with that."

Lee Junior was mourning Leslie in his own way. He bought up every pink rose he could find in Greenville, South Carolina, and had them delivered to the funeral home. He was asked by Leslie's family to be a pallbearer, and he helped deliver Leslie to the mausoleum where she now rests.

She was, Lee Junior told *48 Hours* producers Abra Potkin and Joanna Cetera, quite simply the love of his life.

Napa detectives told Amy that they had spoken to the Youngbloods once, but, based on her information, they would be visiting them again. "I didn't know this, but they didn't get DNA from the first time they visited them, and they're going to get it on this trip," she said.

"Do you feel like Lee Senior is a suspect?" Amy asked the detective.

According to Amy, the detective was blunt, "In my mind, he is."

"I'm not pinning anything on anybody," Amy said, "but I go through different scenarios in my head and, yes, he's a suspect in my head."

Detectives Shulman and Piper visited him in South Carolina. "They treated me with respect," Lee Senior said. "I answered their questions as openly as I could. I wanted to catch the son of a bitch."

Lee Senior, however, had an alibi for Halloween night. In fact, his phone calls (and the subsequent records) to Leslie were proof positive that he was nowhere near Napa.

"They [the police] told me flat out with my monetary situation I could have hired someone to do it. I told them that was bullshit. They were grasping at straws," Lee Senior said.

"I asked them, 'Are you saying I'm a suspect?' They said, 'Everybody's a suspect.' "

When they heard the story of Lee Senior's seeming obsession with Leslie, a lot of people wondered if he'd been the one sending her cash and why. But Lee Senior said it wasn't him, although he does admit to giving Leslie an envelope stuffed with either $250 or $500 in cash on Christmas Day, 2003. He said it was just part of Christmas at the Youngblood house and that other family members got envelopes filled with cash as well. The money, Lee said, was to be used for that family cruise they all took over the New Year's holiday. In addition, Youngblood said he presented Leslie with a television and a DVD/VHS player and recorder.

What had happened on that cruise to change Leslie's mind about marrying Lee? No one seemed to have the answer.

There was so much smoke swirling around Lee Youngblood, Sr. that even Amy wondered aloud whether he could possibly have hired someone to kill Leslie. It seemed far-fetched, but Napa detectives were looking at all the angles, and it might fit into some previous information they'd received—a report of a cab dropping off a man in the area of Dorset Street the night of the murder.

THIRTY-TWO

Something about Harry

Police reporter Marsha Dorgan of the *Napa Valley Register* likes to say that she works for the only newspaper in town, but that's not really true. It's only true if you completely discount the weekly *Napa Valley Sentinel,* which is run by a longtime Napa resident named Harry Martin. Martin, a native of San Francisco, has been around Napa for about twenty years, and even though as a city councilman he's part of the establishment, he considers himself an outsider. Politically, he's enrolled as a member of the Green Party, but that's only out of convenience. Realistically, he's every bit the Independent, which is exactly how he runs his newspaper. When he ran for mayor of Napa back in

2005, a group of high-rollers became so concerned he might possibly win that they formed Citizens for a Sustainable Napa and made it very clear that in their view, having Harry Martin as mayor would be a disaster.

The lead to the story about the group in the more conventional *Register* went like this: "The prospect of Harry Martin wearing the dual hats of Napa City mayor and *Napa Sentinel* publisher was enough to spook a large number of people to open up their wallets for his opponent."

The group considered Martin "divisive." His response? He threatened to start publishing the weekly *Sentinel* two or three times a week. Martin lost his run for mayor.

The *Sentinel* is located on Lincoln Avenue just off Highway 29 next to Theresa's Nail Salon, and Martin's office is just inside the front door, right to the left, as they say. His office is a feast for the eyes, and it's unclear where to look first, but wherever you do, it's likely you'll settle on a bust of President Lincoln. There are many in the tiny room, including one giant one that, Martin admitted ruefully, was a mail-order mistake. "I didn't think it would be quite so big," he said.

Martin's also got a bust of Theodore Roosevelt, as well as a fierce-looking American eagle. You kind of get the idea that this is one politi-

cal animal, this Harry Martin. The *Sentinel* offices are small, crowded, and messier than any
college newspaper, with old copies of the *Sentinel* stacked high and wide. Over the years,
Martin's carved out a niche for his paper, probably because it's fiercely independent and somewhat odd, not in that order. Martin made his
bones at the paper by running stories on black
helicopters trolling over Napa. *Napa!* As if. But
it's part of his whole cloaked espionage, "something's going on here but you don't know about
it" shtick. He also has a tendency to mention
that he used to work for *Defense Systems* magazine more than he really needs to. And if that's
not enough to establish his antiestablishment
credentials, then you should know that he was
the coauthor of a thirteen-part series on govern-
ment mind control.

Somehow the newspaper attracts enough
readers and advertisers that Martin can support
an extended family of offspring and grandchil-
dren. He's been married five times but to only
four women, having married his current wife
twice. He has been a journalist everywhere from
Alaska to Australia.

"I've been with this wife thirty-six years, and
we've been divorced seven," he said while chow-
ing down on a patty melt at Baker's Square Res-

taurant, where he and the waitresses are on a first-name basis. For such a radical guy, he's actually kind of soft-spoken and has a fair amount of down-home charm. It's hard to see what everyone is so riled up about.

Maybe it's because Martin presses people's buttons and does it intentionally. He has a small media fiefdom in town. He has a live local call-in show on Monday nights on Channel 28, where he interviews city officials about local problems and skewers those he doesn't like. A lot of his support comes from Napa's blue-collar base, which finds in Martin a kindred spirit because he, too, believes there are issues more important than, say, the quality of last year's Cabernet. He's also buddies with KVON radio maven Jeff Schectman, and the two like to bounce ideas off each other, particularly about the crime of the year in Napa, the double murders on Dorset Street. Eventually, Martin would produce one of the most important and interesting stories about the murders, but that was months away. Martin could be considered a joke except that he has good sources in the Napa police department. In fact, his sources are so good that veteran reporter Marsha Dorgan has been known to complain that he's getting preferential treatment because of his status as a city councilman. Whether that's true or not, some people pay attention to Martin because he does come up with a nugget now and again.

When the murders first happened, Martin told the police that he and his reporters had talked to a cab driver who delivered to them an eerie tip. "What we heard from some of the cab drivers was that they actually picked the man up and brought him to that location at that hour," he said. "They didn't want to talk to the police about it, because there are people throughout the nation who won't talk to law enforcement, but they might talk to a newspaper or a councilman or someone of that nature.

"The cab driver indicated that he'd picked up an individual out in the western area of town and drove him directly to that house around 1:30, 2:00 a.m., about the time this took place."

It was tantalizing if true, particularly because it supported the cops' own operating theory that the murders were targeted. It also jibed with the idea that perhaps someone had hired someone to commit the murders. It was another lead, and the cops were pursuing everything.

THIRTY-THREE

Good News

As the New Year got under way, Arlene Allen finally received some good news. One of her daughter's best friends, Lily Prudhomme, had decided to get married, and the wedding would take place in February. Since Adriane's murder, Arlene had grown increasingly close to Lily, who had worked at the Napa Sanitation District office with Adriane. It was Lily who had organized the candlelight vigil for Adriane a week after her murder, and as it turned out, Adriane's murder became the catalyst for Lily to go ahead and marry her longtime boyfriend, Eric Copple. They were a bit of an odd couple—Lily was gregarious and Eric was quiet—but somehow the relationship worked, and they had finally decided to make it permanent.

"Adriane's death made me reevaluate what's important in life and my family and friends, making sure they know that I love them," she said. "Eric and I both reevaluated. . . . We've been together almost eight years now. It was time to get married."

Lily and Eric, a surveyor with local firm Michel Brooks & Associates, had been planning to get married back in the fall, and the postponement of those plans had been eating away at Lily. "Eric and I were originally planning to get married on November 1, which is the day Adriane ended up dying, and if we had gone through with that wedding, Adriane and Lauren would have been with us in Hawaii that week."

This time, the wedding would take place at St. Mary's Episcopal Church on Third Street in Napa. Eric was very religious—in fact, his family was fundamentalist, and he and Lily sometimes read scripture together, even back in high school—so the ceremony they planned was to be formal. But the reception would be a rollicking good time.

In planning the event, Lily struggled with the decision about how best to honor Adriane. "As far as Adriane's family and friends, we were worried that her absence would be more pronounced if a lot of our mutual friends were there," she said.

Lily didn't know what to do and asked Ben Katz for his advice. Ben was that kind of person, the guy women turned to for advice. You might even say he was the type of nonthreatening guy women feel comfortable around. Lily told Ben her dilemma. "I want to invite Arlene, but should I? I don't want her to feel bad. It might be hard for her," Lily told Ben.

"You should do what feels right for you," Ben said. "This is your wedding. This is the day you're gonna remember the rest of your life. If you want Arlene to be there, invite her."

"I do want her there. I'm going to ask her."

Lily never regretted her decision. "In the end, we decided to go ahead and invite most of them, and it was a really good thing."

Arlene was overjoyed, especially since she had liked Lily from the moment they met back in 2002. At the time, Adriane was living in the apartment she inhabited before moving to Dorset Street, and Lily lived across the street. "I remember one day I drove up to Adriane's little house and parked on the street there," Arlene said. "Before I had even gotten out of the car, Lily had seen me drive up and dashed across the street and introduced herself to me, and I just fell in love with her right then and there. There was something about her that reminded me so much of Adriane, her pure spirit, her beautiful smile, her love of life.

"Adriane was very forthcoming. She had a very strong sense of right and wrong. If she felt someone was mistreating someone, she would jump right in and defend them. And yet she always had a sparkle in her eye and always had a big smile. You could tell that she really loved life. And Lily reminds me so much of that, too. She is sheer joy to be around."

And that feeling only deepened after Adriane's death. Arlene had taken to calling Lily for lunch whenever she was in Napa, and they'd picked up the friendship Adriane had begun. "I wanted to be there, I really love her," Arlene said. "She was such a part of Adriane's life, and, as such, she's been a big part of my life."

The wedding was a big relief to Arlene; she was desperately in need of something positive. It came in the middle of a long, rainy winter without her beloved Adriane, and Arlene was overjoyed. "They had talked about it, and because of Adriane's death, they really felt sure they shouldn't wait," Arlene remembered. "They felt that you need to live your life and not wait, not hold back. To take every day and live it to the fullest."

Lily even invited Arlene to be part of the church ceremony, and when the day came, Arlene addressed the couple with a passage from the Song of Solomon, the one that deals with love and death and the power of love to go on. She looked them both in the eyes and said, "Love is stronger than death, passion stronger than the grave."

Later, at the reception, Lily dedicated the Maroon 5 song "She Will Be Loved" to Adriane. "We danced to it, and it kind of felt like she was there," Lily said. "She certainly would have been there and a huge part of it if she was alive."

Ben Katz, Adriane's closest male friend, sat at a table with Arlene and Adriane's sister Lexi. Lauren Meanza was invited also but couldn't make it; instead, she sent the couple a card that said, "I wish I could be there, and I know that Adriane will be there."

Lily cherished the card. "I know she's been going through a lot," she said. "She's been doing interviews with the police and just saying her story over and over and over again. I know she's upset deep down, but at this point, she can say the whole thing without crying. She said she had been through it so many times.

"I hope they find whoever did this," Lily said. "I want justice for my friend. It's not gonna make much difference in our lives, because we'd still be without Adriane and Leslie, but it's important. It's important to find out who did this and to find out why. In some sick way, I want to know. I want to know how it happened. I want to know what happened. It's this morbid curiosity. This was my friend. I want to know what happened to her.

"It's been like a horror film, but to have something like this happen in real life and to be so close, you know? She's my friend, one step away. It's weird."

THIRTY-FOUR

The Miller's Daughter

Lily and Eric's wedding might have been a day of joy for Arlene and others, but the Napa detectives hardly noticed. They were seemingly stymied in Napa. None of the leads was turning into anything. They'd located the source of the rumor about the cab driver and decided it was more misinformation than anything. There was only one place to go: back east to visit more of Leslie's former boyfriends. One popular theory—which cops could not discount—was that one of Leslie's ex-boyfriends had held a murderous grudge. Leslie was a special woman, special enough, perhaps, that someone would kill her rather than let another man have her.

Leslie's friend Kelly McCorkle admitted,

"Leslie is a heartbreaker. She never did it on purpose, but I think that there were lot of people out there who would have loved to have won her over and claimed her as their girlfriend, but Leslie was a free spirit."

Leslie's brother PJ, though mostly supportive of his sister's boyfriends, was having second thoughts. "Some of them even came to the funeral. I just kind of wonder in the back of my mind if they had something to do with this or not. I would like to have the peace of mind to know that it wasn't any of them so we can move on beyond that."

Leslie's mother, Cathy, completely discounted the involvement of any of Leslie's old boyfriends, "because when she would break up with a boyfriend, they were still friends. I mean, it's not like she left a chain of enemies."

But the police couldn't afford to take Cathy's word for it; they continued to check old boyfriends, including three who had fallen particularly hard for Leslie. One of them was Aaron Davis who had met Leslie when they were both working in Seward, Alaska, in the summer of 1998. It was an old romance, but it had never cooled off completely for Aaron. When police searched Leslie's computer, they discovered that Aaron had just located Leslie again; in fact, their first exchange in years had occurred just weeks before she was murdered. Aaron had tracked Leslie down through the Miss Williamston beauty pageant. His e-mail reached Renee Tollison, who passed it along to Leslie. Leslie was glad to hear from him, according to Amy Brown.

"She said, 'You'll never guess who I got an e-mail from.' "

Amy guessed, and Leslie said, "He e-mailed me, and I e-mailed him back. He's doing fine, he just wanted to know where I was and what I was doing. It was really great getting to talk with him again."

"I never felt Aaron had anything to do with this," Amy said. "I think it was just a coincidence."

But the cops could not just write it off to chance, at least not until they investigated.

Leslie and Aaron had met back in the summer of 1999 in Alaska, when Leslie was working in her mother's bakery. She was twenty, and Aaron was twenty-four, and they both were Southerners who found themselves thousands of miles from home, living in tiny Seward, a beautiful town on Resurrection Bay and home to about 3,000 people tops in the summers. Leslie's mother had moved there to open a bakery with a friend. Leslie was still a student at UGA, but each summer, she dutifully headed west to work with her mother at the Miller's Daughter bakery and café. Leslie did some baking and prepared lunch for the locals. The bakery had a prime location, right next to the marina, and it became a popular choice for good, inexpensive food.

Aaron, who now is bald and wears a goatee, was up there working on a charter fishing boat, and he couldn't help but be taken by his fellow Southerner. "I was in there every day for lunch, and those eyes . . ." He trailed off and looked up dreamily. "I talked to her all the time and finally got her to go out with me."

Pretty soon, he said that he and Leslie were an item. It's clear that Aaron was head over heels in love. To this day, he still refers to Leslie as "the perfect woman."

"She is the most amazing woman I've ever met," he said. "Every girl I meet I compare to her, but she was perfect, everything I was looking for and then some. There are other women out there but not another Leslie—she was perfect."

Speaking of comparisons, the cops were beginning to see that there was no one "type" that Leslie seemed drawn to. Aaron, with his country sincere manner, is the polar opposite of Lee Youngblood Jr., who is far more slick and sophisticated. And neither of them, apparently, can hold a candle to Donald, the tall, hunky firefighter who was Leslie's neighbor in Napa. But far from home in Alaska, Leslie became friendly with Aaron, though friends say it was probably just a summer fling. The two would go out on dinner cruises, where Aaron still fondly recalls Leslie snuggling up to him. "She'd just wrap up in my jacket and sit there lying on my shoulder and talk," he said. "To me, she was the one. I know it. I swear it. It didn't matter what was going on with her. If there was something wrong and she saw you down in the dumps, she would bring you up. She was always positive."

Aaron would do anything if it pleased Leslie and went out of his way to make sure she was happy. Leslie loved a folk singer named Hobo Jim, who is to Alaska what Jack Johnson is to Hawaii. Hobo Jim played at the Yukon Bar in Seward every Sunday and was so popular that the bar is referred to as "the church of Hobo." Every Sunday when Jim was there performing, Aaron would take Leslie. When Hobo Jim once played at Fox Island at a private party, Aaron made sure he and Leslie found a way in. Aaron had it bad and seems the personification of the old Robert Palmer song "Addicted to Love."

Aaron readily admitted that he had hopes of marrying Leslie, who told him she was not ready to settle down. "I was gonna marry that girl, I still had the dream," he said. "She was a heart-breaker, that's for sure."

But Aaron denied that his heart was broken by Leslie. After she left Alaska and returned to school, the two stayed in touch, and when Aaron returned to the mainland, he and Leslie reunited. He would visit her in Atlanta, where they would go see the Braves play baseball, and she would visit him in his hometown of Columbia, Tennessee. "Whenever we were together, we just had a blast," he said.

He often referred to her as his Georgia peach and said that in the aftermath of her death, he saves every Georgia and South Carolina quarter he has ever found, just as a small reminder of the woman who turned his life upside down.

But the visits, e-mails, and phone calls fell off, and by October 2004, Aaron wasn't even sure how to get in touch with Leslie anymore. That's when he contacted Renee Tollison and wound up reconnecting with Leslie. The cops found that the e-mails between the two seemed harmless despite Aaron's obvious fascination with the former beauty queen. They took his DNA and waited for the results before taking it any farther.

Aaron, they thought, seemed heartsick by Leslie's death but hardly someone who wanted her dead.

THIRTY-FIVE

Mortalitas

During college, Leslie had met a lot of good-looking young men, but not too many had the single-mindedness of Grant East, who was yet another in a long line of men who felt as though they had to have her, and he made sure Leslie knew it. "Leslie went into every relationship with an open heart, to see how the man would treat her, whether he was ready to make a commitment," said Amy Brown. "And that's the way it was with Grant, but he just fell in love with Leslie. He bought her a car."

Amy was flabbergasted. It wasn't a new car—it was a teal-colored '93 Ford Explorer—but he bought it for Leslie after they'd been going out for only about three months. "That's just what guys would do for Leslie," Amy said. "She didn't ask for a car. Leslie's car was having some problems, and she was saying she needed to get a new one. One day they went shopping for it, and she was going to get a loan, but she couldn't get it, and he went out and took the loan out for her. So basically he bought her a car."

Amy sat Leslie down and said, "This is crazy. This is crazy. You don't even know if this is the man you're going to be with. You can't take gifts this large from somebody."

Vanessa Schnurr agreed with Amy and told Leslie so. "I remember driving in that car and telling her she couldn't keep it. At the time Grant gave it to her, she was losing interest, and it was an effort on his part to make sure she kept him around."

If that was his intention, it didn't work. Vanessa even drove with Leslie to the bank, where she asked that her name be taken off the loan. Soon the car was history, and so was Grant.

But it seems Grant wasn't completely ready to give Leslie up, not by a long shot. He went one step further than any of the other men Leslie knew: he built a Web site in her honor. Grant's Web site (since taken down) features a photograph of Leslie in an extremely low-cut black evening dress. Next to her photo, Grant wrote this: "Leslie Mazzara, the young lady to the left, recently was crowned Miss Williamston, South Carolina. I'd like to say more, but I don't know where to start."

Beneath that statement and to the right of Leslie's photo is a poem by Robert Frost called "The Silken Tent." It begins: "She is as in a field a silken tent, at midday when a sunny summer breeze."

Another page of the Web site features an icon of a gleeful-looking skeleton with this: "Mortalitas. The adventures of a graduate student in Spanish at the University of Georgia." None of it would seem particularly odd or heinous, except in light of Leslie's death. Vanessa dismissed the Web site as "a school project" Grant forgot to take down after a computer class ended.

Amy agreed. "Grant was more of a drama king, but I don't think the Web site meant anything, because I knew Grant and his personality. He loved Leslie. It [building a Web site to Leslie] is not a normal thing to do— at least not for normal people—but because I knew Grant and his personality, it didn't strike me as anything. I know that he idolized her.

He was very proud of her when she won Miss Williamston, and I think that's the picture he put on there."

It may not have struck Amy as weird, but it did to a lot of other people. Steve Huff, the guru of true crime bloggers who follows true crime stories with a passion Dominick Dunne can only envy, seized upon the Grant East Web site back in April 2005.

He posted his thoughts on the Cybersleuths. com message board:

Look—I'm not saying that this is the guy, at all, but I was struck by [the Grant East Web site] . . . In photos elsewhere on the site, which it looks like he stopped constructing mid-stream, the guy looks like a very handsome, presentable, fresh-faced sort of dude. He doesn't mention Leslie anywhere else but that page, either.

Here is why I found the site striking:

- It's name is Mortalitas. That's Latin, for the state of being mortal, or death, a dying.
- Witness the main page of the site. There's a strange-looking skeleton in a dance pose. It may be utterly insignificant, but I'll note for the record that Leslie was a dancer. That was the talent she used in that portion of beauty pageants.

- The poem used is a strangely abstract one for someone you are in love with, or attracted to—Robert Frost's "The Silken Tent."

Here's my point, which is not necessarily that Mr. East should be under any suspicion; if she inspired such a reaction in him, for reasons we've yet to know—and I point out too that on the page with the Frost poem East refers to her as "The lady on the left"—her photo on the left side of the page—as if he might not even know her all that well—but if she inspired such a reaction in him, who else responded to Leslie this way? The page devoted to her is either an indication of love, and he was a boyfriend, or it is an indication of obsession. The women I've known personally who have developed stalker problems have sometimes had this happen more than once. To be frank, on the opposite end of the spectrum, I've been stalked more than once, too, and I would never be mistaken for *GQ* material. Anyone can get stalked, but my experience has made me feel that certain people will get it more than others, as I've already had more than my fair share. Often these people may be attractive, and also very accessible and easy to know. I wonder if besides "attractive" being obviously applicable to Leslie, she was also very kind, open, and easy to know. If so, then surely more than one guy, being the way some men are, got the wrong idea about her friendliness. There are men in the world, and as I've found, women too, who will mistake warm conversation for come-ons.

In short—if she could inspire Grant East to put a poem with her picture, making her seem like poetry to him, who else did she inspire? Who else developed a habit of thinking about Leslie? If they were the sort who was prone already to fantasy, to having relationships with others that were mostly in their own heads (part and parcel of the stalker mindset—the two who stalked me thought there was much, much more to our relationships than there was), then who is to say that they did not target Leslie that night and take out Adriane when she tried to aid her friend?

Again, I cannot legitimately support this line of thinking too far without much more to go on than I have. I just finally clarified for myself why Grant East's page about Leslie has stuck with me.

Was it all just the work of another guy obsessed with Leslie or something more? Napa detectives decided to find out.

THIRTY-SIX

Off on Her Own Adventure

Mac McClellion remembered the first time he saw Leslie Mazzara. It was right after she was crowned Miss Williamston in the summer of 2002. Leslie was in a local coffee shop in Anderson, her hometown, collecting money for the Stephanie Carter home, the home for abused kids named after the four-year-old girl who was killed.

"I remember walking in, and she had this smile that was just unbelievable. I stopped breathing, but I don't know if it was because I wanted to suck in my gut or because she was just that beautiful." He laughed. "I wanted to talk to her, but I didn't know how to. I guess I was just scared. She looked intimidating based on how beautiful she was. But then . . . I was holding my nephew at the time, and she came over to see my nephew and we talked."

Leslie cooed a bit over the boy and told Mac that she was raising money for the Stephanie fund, and he dropped $100 into her collection box, just like that. He also got her phone number. "And then a couple of days later, I got enough courage up to call her to see if she wanted to go out, and, surprising to me, she said yes. She was just so approachable."

Mac, a recent college graduate, became her boyfriend and one of her family's favorites. They'd always wished Leslie would just settle down with Mac. "We just started hanging out, and I had a great time whenever I was around her. We became really good friends, and at the end of the summer, she was going back to Georgia and I was coming back down to Columbia. She had another year of school, and I was starting law school."

The two stayed in touch and developed a great friendship, according to Mac. "Everything just kind of blossomed when we first started seeing each other, and it never stopped, just got better every time I saw her."

Mac agrees with everyone's assessment of Leslie. "Leslie was just a great overall person in general. There's really not enough words to describe how good she was. I never heard anyone say anything bad about her; she was just that type of person. And it might be a cliché, but she was the type of woman that every man wanted to be with."

But their budding romance was upset by timing. They were at different points in their lives. Mac was just beginning to go to school again, and Leslie was about to graduate. She was still "being Leslie," and he was looking to get a little more settled. They were living in different cities when Leslie met Lee Junior and began living with him. "I don't really wanna say we broke up," Mac said, but then he caught himself and said, "Well, I guess we did. She didn't know exactly what she wanted to do, and she was kind of searching for herself."

Mac stayed friendly with Leslie while she was living with Lee Youngblood Jr. straight through the breakup. Then, in spring of 2004, she asked Mac out to dinner. "She told me she was going to go to California for the summer," he said.

"You're gonna stay out there longer," he told Leslie. "You're gonna get out there, you're gonna enjoy it, and you're gonna stay."

"No," she insisted. "No, no, no. I'm not gonna stay."

Mac didn't believe her and was not surprised when she called him at the end of that summer. "Mac," Leslie said, "I think I wanna stay awhile longer."

"I knew it," he said now. "She was out there on an adventure, trying to find herself. She loved her job. She was getting a promotion, and that made her happy. The sales position was something she really wanted. I encouraged her to stay out there as long as she thought she needed to."

Mac said he desperately wanted her to come back to South Carolina and be with him but thought she needed to get California out of her system. "I didn't want to tell her to come back because I missed her and have her come back to me but be miserable. I wish I would have now," he said quietly.

The shock of his life came when the cops began combing through Leslie's cell-phone calling numbers at random to see who answered. It was Election Day, November 2, and Mac was coming back from voting. His cell phone rang, and he saw it was Leslie calling. They had a little catchphrase, so Mac initiated it when he answered.

"Hey man!"

A woman said hello, but it wasn't Leslie. It

was someone saying she worked for the Napa police. She began asking Mac a bunch of questions relating to Leslie, and he finally asked, "Why are you asking me these questions? What is this all about?"

She told him Leslie had been killed over the weekend. Mac felt physically sick. "I had to pull over to the side of the road," he said. "It didn't make sense, like someone was playing a horrible joke on me. I kept saying, 'No, this can't be true.'"

Ten minutes later, Mac's father called and asked if he'd heard the news. "And that's when it hit me. I was, like, 'Wow.'

"The funeral was the worst, because that's when it really hit me. Leslie was gone. I'm never going to be able to talk with her again. For weeks after, I was hoping that her name would pop up on my cell phone . . ."

Afterward, Mac wrote a letter to the editor of the *Anderson Independent*, a letter attempting to inform those who had never met Leslie how special she was. It began, "Have you ever attempted to describe the beauty of a rainbow to someone who's never had the gift of sight?"

It's hard for Mac to think about Leslie dying and the way she died. He much prefers to remember the good times, like when he visited

Leslie in California and she wanted to go skydiving, which was typical of her adventurous spirit. He has a photo of her free-falling in the sky, and it's a photo her mother, Cathy, particularly likes because it shows Leslie's spirit. "I remember that day," he said. "She went up first, and I promised I would go up, too, if she did. They took me down to the landing site, and I was waiting for her to come on down, and I heard her start screaming about 3,000 feet up in the air. And she's just screaming at the top of her lungs, just laughing, and I could see this little dot up in the sky, and I can hear her yelling. And I remember her landing. She let out a big laugh and said, 'That is so cool!' I just remember that to this day, and it's one of my greatest memories of her. She was always happy, but she was especially happy that day.

"It's so hard to imagine I'll never see her again, never be able to talk to her again."

When the police from Napa came to see him, Mac did not hesitate for one second before allowing them to take a DNA sample from him. "I've got nothing to hide," he said. "I know I had nothing to do with this crime."

THIRTY-SEVEN

The Raising Race

By the middle of August 2005, the families of Adriane and Leslie had heard only generalities from the police, who were in a tough spot. They wanted to be forthcoming with the families, but they also were trying to build a case that would have a successful prosecution and didn't want anyone leaking information, even family members. Their interests were competing ones. As a result, the families still knew almost nothing of what was going on behind the scenes and just a few details of the crime itself. With the summer more than halfway over, the one-year anniversary of the double murders would be upon them, and the intruder and murderer was still at large.

It seemed to the families that the investigation was at a standstill, and Leslie's brothers were growing impatient.

Leslie's twenty-seventh birthday was August 1, and her family spent it in quiet remembrance. The one thing they were looking forward to was a plan hatched by Kelly McCorkle, who was determined to do something in Leslie's memory. Three weeks after Leslie's death, Kelly had left to compete in the around-the-world CBS program *The Amazing Race,* where she met Rob Mariano and Amber Brkich of *Survivor* fame, who were also on the show that season. Inspired by her experience on the program, Kelly created a similar type of race and scavenger hunt in Anderson, South Carolina. All the proceeds would go toward Leslie's favorite charity, the Calvary Home for Children.

During her life, Leslie had raised money for Stephanie's Cottage, the home for abused children on the property. Now Kelly had convinced the charity that there should be a cottage named after Leslie, and she was dedicated to making it happen with the race she dubbed "The Raising Race."

To help her raise money and draw a crowd, Kelly called on some of her friends from *The Amazing Race* to make guest appearances.

Even Rob and Amber, that ubiquitous couple, showed up, as did hundreds of competitors. It's brutally hot in South Carolina in August, but the competitors took to the streets with great gusto, urged on by Kelly and her celebrity friends. "It's all about Leslie," Kelly said. "I wanted to turn something tragic into something positive."

Leslie's mother, Cathy, flew in to be there for the race and seemed overwhelmed at the outpouring of support. "There's no way to make meaning out of losing my daughter, but I'm so proud of Kelly and my son and those who worked so hard to make this happen, and I have real hope that Leslie's Cottage will be built," she said. "We need to create awareness of child abuse, and this is a step. There's not much that can help with the pain of losing a child, but every night before you go to bed, hug your child and tell them you love them. Nothing more important in the world than that.

"Leslie told me many times that she knew she was loved. She never didn't feel loved, and that's a great comfort I have right now. If that is the legacy she leaves, that children should be loved, then I could have some peace with that. She had this wonderful joy for life."

* * *

When Arlene remembered the good times with Adriane, she thought about the many days and nights the two spent watching their beloved San Francisco Giants. They were diehard fans, and being at the ballpark always made Arlene happy. "You can't be depressed at the ballpark," she said.

Sue McHugh, a *48 Hours* producer, had grown close to Arlene in the course of reporting the story. It's inevitable, really. Producers often spend months on a story, and the bond between subject and journalist often gets quite close. It was the same with Arlene and McHugh, who began to confide in each other.

48 Hours Mystery was sticking with the story, despite the lack of a resolution, and had decided that the best approach would be to highlight the unsolved nature of the case and appeal to viewers to come forward if they had any information. As McHugh listened closely to Arlene in interviews and over lunches and dinners, she thought it might be best to get her mind off Adriane's death a bit, so she invited Arlene to a ballgame in San Francisco.

Arlene, a veteran at obtaining good tickets, told McHugh where to go on the Giants Web site, and before long, they were sitting right behind home plate. It seemed like good karma, and they had a great time at the game, which had one exciting play after another. The Giants beat their rivals the Oakland A's 3–2, and the game was all you could ask for.

Arlene and McHugh were basking in the afterglow of the game and walking to their car when they ran into Lily, her husband, Eric, and Lily's parents. More good karma, thought McHugh, and what a night. She was pleased, and Arlene was excited, and the little group chatted about the game.

The night ended on a high, just as McHugh had hoped.

THIRTY-EIGHT

Kelly on Dorset Street

As part of the production for the *48 Hours Mystery* broadcast on the murders, the producers asked Kelly to visit the Dorset Street home where her best friend, Leslie, had been murdered. The idea was to allow her to see the house while the cameras were rolling, a visit that almost guaranteed emotion, a valuable commodity on television. The producers had fallen in love with Kelly as a character who could make Leslie's memory come alive. They decided she would be the voice that would carry viewers through the story and, they hoped, make them feel how special these two young women were. Kelly agreed, mostly out of curiosity. After being inseparable since they were teenagers, Kelly and Leslie had been apart for the six months Leslie had lived in Napa, and Kelly was more than a little curious about what the house looked like.

Kelly had not been having an easy time of it since her friend's death. She felt very uncomfortable going to sleep, and she often had nightmares that she or her sister was being chased by a man intent on killing one or both. And then there was her own living situation. Kelly lived in Washington, D.C., in an identical roommate situation to the one Leslie had had in Napa. In Kelly's house, as in Leslie's, one roommate lived downstairs and two upstairs. The first night Kelly returned to her D.C. house after Leslie's funeral, it was 7:00 and dark, and no one was home. She stood outside, unable to go in.

She called her mother and told her, "I can't go inside."

Her mother reassured her, "You're safer inside than outside."

"I can't, I can't go inside."

But she found the courage to do it.

Kelly found herself living her life differently from before, more cautiously. "I've always wanted to be real careful, but this just made me more aware about meeting strangers," she said. "When you're shaking someone's hand and you have no clue that they're going to follow you home and do something with you or try to kill you that night."

She had to shake herself out of her irrational fears. "It's just wild. I think Leslie would be mad if I lived my life looking over my shoulder thinking that someone is coming after me. She would just want me not to take anything for granted, and, more than anything, that's what I've learned."

The day Kelly visited Leslie's Napa house became an incredibly emotional journey both for Kelly and for the producers.

Driving to the house, Kelly began to think more and more about what had gone on that night. "I just fear for what she went through," Kelly said. "I just hope and pray that she did not wake up with somebody standing over her attacking her."

Kelly began to cry as the memories got stronger. "I just want to protect her. I just want to run to her, and it's so hard to think that somebody so sweet and loving and innocent went through something so tragic and so hard. Even to this day, I feel like I don't want to believe it happened. I just keep telling myself, even now, 'This didn't happen. This didn't happen.'"

At the house, Kelly continued to think about

what had happened there. Walking through the rooms, she touched a wall and said a prayer to herself. She knew there would not be blood everywhere but couldn't help thinking about it. "I just had this fear of walking in and seeing blood everywhere, this horror scene.

"It was like a horror movie, and to think that she experienced that firsthand and lived through that is just unimaginable. . . . Right after it happened, I was really hurting, and a coroner's wife, who's good friends with our family, came and talked to my family about stab wounds and people who lived through stabbings, and they informed me that a lot of research had been done, and they said there's not a lot of pain, that people go through shock, that they don't feel it, and those are things that really kind of helped me cope. I just didn't want her to hurt. I didn't want her to feel pain, and so it was good for me to know that maybe she didn't feel that way.

"But the hardest thing is: I know she felt the fear."

Kelly began crying and took a break, only to remember a dream she'd had. "Right after it happened," she said, "I dreamed that I could see it happening to her and I couldn't get to her and

I couldn't help her, and then I dreamed that I was being chased and stabbed and I couldn't save myself. It's like I live this nightmare every day since it happened. It's a nightmare just living and knowing that this happened to her."

Kelly couldn't help but put herself in Lauren's shoes and wonder what she would have done had she been living in the house and heard the screams of her roommate. "It's hard to say what Lauren should have done, because I don't think anybody knows how they would react until they're in that situation, but I play out all these scenarios: Is it better for me to call the police right now? Is it better for me to go upstairs? I think that I probably would have grabbed a weapon myself. A bat, a knife, something, and gone up there and tried to help and tried to fight. It is the ultimate nightmare. You're not sitting in a movie theater anymore."

Like everyone else, Kelly was surprised at how small the house was. "You can reach out your arm and touch Adriane's door, and you can reach out your arm this way and touch Leslie's door. They were that close to each other." Walking into Leslie's bedroom, Kelly said, "I just keep thinking, this is the last place that she was. This is the last place that she was, and I just want to breathe it in. I just want to have her right here, beside me.

"When I walk in her room and see where her bed must have been, I just want to lie down in it. I just want to be close to her . . . again."

THIRTY-NINE

CSI: Florida

Some 3,000 miles from Napa, there was important work going on in the case that the public was unaware of. It was lab work, and it was going on behind closed doors at a company called DNAPrint Geonomics in Sarasota, Florida. Scientists at the lab had put on a seminar at the California Homicide Investigators Association, and someone from the Napa police department had attended. The lab had come up with a technique unusual in DNA analysis. With a DNA sample such as blood, the lab was able to tell not only if the donor was male or female but also what his or her ancestry was.

Dr. Matt Thomas, senior scientist and laboratory manager, explained that traditionally, DNA is useful when you have another sample to compare it to. Comparing the two samples side-by-side, a scientist can tell whether the DNA is a likely match or whether a person can be excluded from being the donor. That's why in a lot of rape cases, you're likely to hear that the chances of two people having the same DNA is one in a million or some extraordinary number. Basically, what the scientist is saying is "that's a match," because the odds are against two people having that exact strand of DNA.

But what if you have nothing to compare your DNA sample to? "If you have nobody to compare it to, it doesn't do much good," Dr. Thomas said.

So far, the Napa cops had successfully eliminated nearly all of Adriane's and Leslie's current and former boyfriends. On paper, some of them appeared to be suspects and some appeared to have motive, but none of that mattered. The DNA didn't match. None of the more than 200 men who willingly gave police their DNA had been a match.

Correspondent Bill Lagattuta put the question directly to Detective Todd Shulman. "I just want to make clear one point," Lagattuta said. "Of all the boyfriends, ex-boyfriends, men that Leslie was involved with that you know of, you have been able to clear them all?"

Shulman answered with a definitive yes.

Shulman did hedge on one point. He said that while all the men had been cleared by their own DNA, it did not mean one of them didn't hire someone else to kill the women. Lagattuta pounced: "Are you implying that this could've been a murder for hire?"

"It's a possible theory that someone paid someone else to go in there and commit these crimes," Shulman said, but added, "but the violent nature of the crime I don't think is indicative of that type of thing at all."

It was frustrating. The cops at that point had collected a lot of DNA samples and had interviewed more than 1,200 people. Napa cops had plugged their sample into the existing DNA databanks but came up empty, meaning that the killer either did not have a criminal record or that his DNA had never been taken for whatever reason. They were at a dead end until they heard the seminar conducted by Dr. Thomas and company.

"We can tell you what group the sample is most likely descended from," he said. "The test breaks down the sample into its relative affiliation. We're talking about three groups: sub-Saharan African, European, and Asian."

It seemed worth a try. The lab had had some other successes. They helped break the case of the

Louisiana serial killer by telling the cops the killer was most likely black, and they had helped cops in Mamouth Lakes, California, test the remains of a woman found on the outskirts of town. The cops had thought the woman was Asian, but a test by DNAPrint Genomics revealed that she was 100 percent Native American.

By the end of the summer of 2005, the lab sent its results back to Napa. The killer's ancestry, the test had determined, was 96 percent northern European and 4 percent southeastern European. What's more, the lab told cops that "with 85 percent certainty," they believed the killer had blue or green eyes. The ancestry information was important because it was clear now that the killer was not Latino. It was a small piece of information, but it was something. The theory that possibly an immigrant worker had killed the women and had hot-footed it to Mexico was just not viable.

And as it turned out, the ancestry analysis was not the most important lab work done for the cops. Another piece of evidence had been sent to the Justice Department back in January, and it, too, was coming to fruition here in August.

This piece would give the cops the clue they needed to break the case.

FORTY

New Evidence

Word of some new evidence first reached the ears of *Sentinel* publisher Harry Martin. He'd heard from his sources that the cops were going from store to store, gas station to gas station, asking about a particular brand of cigarettes. "The cops were asking who bought these cigarettes, but the people who told us about it didn't seem to know anything," Martin said.

The brand the cops were asking about was Camel Turkish Gold. The cigarettes had been sent to the labs at the Justice Department back in the winter of 2005, and the lab had determined that whoever smoked those cigarettes—found in the back and front of the house—was the same male whose blood was inside the house. The DNA was a match. Ever since the Napa forensic investigator had plucked those two butts off the ground on the morning of the killing, the cops were wondering if perhaps the killer had smoked them. Now they knew for a fact that he had.

Investigators scurried to find out more information about Camel Turkish Gold, which had unusual markings on the band, unique markings. "The cigarettes were very distinctive," said lead detective Todd Shulman. "It's a unique brand. It's only been on the market for fourteen months now. And it's not sold in every convenience store you go to. We feel it's a significant lead because the type of cigarette is somewhat specialized."

What's more, the cigarettes, which were smoked down to the filter and found in two locations at the crime scene, indicated something about the killer's mindset: he was not in a hurry to do what he wound up doing. "It shows someone who had time to be there, and yet he was thinking about what he was gonna be doing," Shulman theorized. "Maybe working up the courage to do it. Or again, it could be someone who's very deliberate, who is thinking through his thoughts and through his plans that he's already made in his mind of what he's gonna do when he gets into the house."

Not only had the killer taken his time before going into the house, but he had also moved around it, front to back or vice versa. One cigarette butt was found on the ground in the rear yard, and the other was collected in the gutter at the driveway in front of the residence. It certainly seemed the killer had been casing the house, trying to figure out the best way to get in.

There were other clues to be gleaned from the cigarettes themselves. The short time they were on the market might also mean something, according to Shulman. "People who smoke cigarettes are very brand-conscious, and they like a particular flavor of cigarettes, and certain kinds of people are very loyal to certain kinds of cigarettes. So you're thinking, is it someone who was a Camel smoker and just switched to this particular new brand of Camel? Is it someone who's a new smoker and maybe is trying this out? All these kinds of things are going through your mind, thinking of the 'what ifs' of who this person could be."

Harry Martin was right on the money with the information he'd been hearing. The cops were out canvassing convenience stores, Shulman said, "first to determine if they even sold that brand and then to talk to the store owners and the people who work there, see if they've sold those types of cigarettes to anybody they can recall."

The only problem was, they were not having any luck. When they did find a store that carried the brand, the owner didn't remember anything about the person who bought them.

But Shulman was determined not to stop there.

FORTY-ONE

Do You Know Anyone Who Smokes?

Before the police released news of the cigarettes to the public, they ran it by Lauren Meanza. Whenever police thought they might have a solid lead, they checked with Lauren to see if it jogged her memory. Asking her about the Camel Turkish Gold cigarettes was nothing new. They had been leaning on Lauren for information for months. This time, investigators wanted to know if she remembered which of their friends smoked, especially someone who might have been in the house.

At first, Lauren said no, she couldn't recall anyone, but then she had a subconscious memory of people smoking in the house. Thinking about it some more, she realized she was thinking of Lily Prudhomme and her new husband, Eric Copple. Both had helped move Adriane into the house, and she seemed to remember that both of them smoked. What brand she had no idea, since she was not a smoker herself.

Had the cops questioned Eric? she asked. Had they gotten his DNA and ruled him out? The detective checked out his database while Lauren stayed on the phone. Nope, nothing on Eric Copple; somehow, he had slipped under the radar.

On September 7, Detective Shulman called Lily at the Napa Sanitation District and asked for Eric's phone number. She told him that Eric had taken a new job at Brooks & Associates in Yountville. Eric was out in the field, as he often was, since he was employed as a surveyor. Shulman left a message with the secretary asking Eric to give him a call.

Two weeks went by before Shulman realized he had not heard back from Eric. It was then September 22, and the department was getting ready to release the information to the public. Shulman this time left a message on Eric's home answering machine; he'd gotten the number from Lily when he'd originally called on September 7.

Later in the day on September 22, the police released the news about the DNA on the cigarettes matching the blood inside the house and the unique brand. Fingers crossed, they were hoping for the best. If nothing else, it was the first new information about the crime released in a long time, and reporter Marsha Dorgan jumped on it and played it big in the *Napa Valley Register*.

"We think that this little piece of information added in will prompt someone in the public to give us information, to call in with tips that they may have," Shulman said.

They sat back and waited.

FORTY-TWO

A Confession

Five days later, on September 27, 2005, Commander Jeff Troendly had quit for the day and had gone across the street to work out at a local gym. Before heading home, he stopped in his office to answer a few e-mails. He was in his car in the police parking lot, about to leave, when another officer pulled his car up beside Troendly's.

"Where are you going?"

"Home."

"You might wanna rethink that. Some people just walked in, and one of 'em says he killed Adriane Insogna and Leslie Mazzara."

Troendly figured it was a psycho or some poor slob confessing to get attention. It happened all the time. "Shut up."

"No, I mean it. This seems legit."

"Are you kidding?"

"Nope, and you know what else? I don't think you're going home tonight."

Troendly hustled back inside.

At around the same time, Sergeant Tim Cantillon placed a call to the home of Detective Shulman.

"Hey, you better get down here. There's a guy says he killed those two girls on Dorset Street. Figured you'd wanna do the interview."

"I'll be right there."

In minutes, Troendly and Shulman were huddled together at the station. Sitting in the hallway was the alleged killer's family, pacing nervously. The cops ignored them. They knew the suspect had waived his rights and was spilling his guts to Officer Russ Davis, a member of the gang unit. Troendly and Shulman went to a room next to the interrogation room, where they could watch what was going on. A camera was beaming back everything on a closed-circuit monitor.

The person being questioned was someone none of them expected. What's more, he had walked into the police station carrying a pack of

Camel Turkish Golds. The interrogation went on for hours, and the cops took turns, first Davis, then Shulman, and finally Troendly. Troendly in particular wanted to know the motive, but he left the room unsatisfied. "It just doesn't add up," he said later. "Something's missing. He's holding something back."

But motive was something the district attorney did not have to prove in court. More important to the police was that this suspect knew a lot of things that had never before been revealed to the public.

It looked as if they had their man.

PART THREE

The Confession

FORTY-THREE

An Arrest

At 11:15 that night, Arlene Allen received a call from the Napa detectives. They knew she was desperate for any scrap of information about her daughter's murderer, and they didn't want her to hear the news first from someone else.

"We've made an arrest in your daughter's murder," the cop told her.

Arlene said she was stunned and unable to speak.

"Who is it? What's his name?" she asked.

"Eric Copple."

Arlene didn't think she'd heard right. Eric Copple? Lily's husband? Why would he kill Adriane and Leslie? And what about Lily? A million thoughts were going through her head.

"I was not at all prepared for the answer to that question," Arlene said. "When I learned who it was, I was shocked, and I was overcome with grief, because this was the then fiancé, now husband, of my daughter's dear friend—my dear friend, too. And I was just overcome with grief for the tragedy that her life now has become and for the tragedy that her family will suffer and that her husband's family will suffer. It just feels like so many lives continue to be shattered by a rash act of four minutes. I look at my family, my brother, my sisters, my mom, we're all twisting in the wind right now and trying to deal with this loss, and I know that Leslie's family is feeling the same way. And now here we have two more families that may not recover from this. It's heartbreaking. I am just so heartbroken over this."

In her bones, Arlene was sure Lily had no idea of her husband's alleged involvement. She couldn't have—Lily had loved Adriane too much.

"Oh, my God, Lily! My heart is broken for her," she said.

She thought about the past eleven months. Eric had been right under their noses the whole time. How was it possible? What did she really know about him? Arlene thought back to the past year. She had sat at the same table as Eric and Lily during a function for the Napa Sanitation District. She had attended Lily and Eric's February wedding. Arlene was part of that wedding and had been to the rehearsal dinner. She had read scripture to them: "Love is stronger than death and passion fierce as the grave." She had looked Eric in the eyes when she'd said it and now remembered that his eyes looked "sad." Before, that had hardly registered, but now it meant everything.

Arlene just knew that Lily must be as shocked as she was. The women had become so close that Lily was nearly her surrogate daughter. Lily had planned the candlelight vigil in Adriane's honor. Lily and Arlene had sat together back in May, when Adriane was honored at the annual If Given a Chance banquet. Lily had made a point of asking to sit with Arlene. The whole thing was just inconceivable.

"This is just devastating," she said. "Lily is a dear friend of mine as well. I don't want to lose her. I want her to know that I love her and will be here for her. I'm just shocked, just like I was when I first found out Adriane was murdered. I haven't slept since I heard the news. It would have been better if it was a stranger. I expected it to be a stranger."

Arlene said she never remembered Adriane saying a bad word about Eric. "Adriane really liked Eric. She would talk about Eric," she said, but admitted that her daughter's fondness for Eric was all wrapped up in her friendship with Lily. "Adriane liked him because Lily loved him. He was part of Lily, therefore Adriane loved him, too."

Leslie's mother, Cathy Harrington, received the call she'd been anticipating at around 2:00 that morning at her home in Ludington, Michigan.

"It was a detective from the Napa police department informing me that they had made an arrest," she said. "It was quite a surprise and a shock. It's hard to explain how you feel when you get that call. I had been waiting for that call for eleven months. I think I'd stopped expecting it. For a while, I couldn't wait for the phone to ring, and every time it would ring, I would think it was the police telling me they had found him, but it didn't happen until now."

Cathy was grateful. She'd been one of the last to know her daughter had been murdered, and she didn't want to go through that again. This time she and Arlene were the first to know of the arrest. The police also had called Lauren Meanza, who, as the only survivor, had been living in fear and in hiding since the murders.

"When I hung up the phone, it was like I could finally exhale," Cathy said. "I think I didn't realize how tense, how I'd almost been holding my breath for eleven months. As I told my son, I don't think I've lived a normal day since November 1, 2004. Whoever this person is, he pretty much shattered our lives as we knew it. We'll never be the same."

Like everyone else, Cathy was curious about Eric, whom she did not know firsthand as Arlene did. "You know what my biggest question is? What happened to this man, this young man, in his life that would make him a murderer? And what is it about our society that continues to breed and create murderers?"

As for the question why, Cathy was not expecting anything rational. "You can't make sense out of a senseless crime," she said. "There's no such thing."

Within hours, Arlene was on the phone to Cathy, apologizing for assuming someone from Leslie's side had committed the murders. She told Cathy she felt relieved and was grieving for Lily. "Somehow Eric was missed," Arlene told

Cathy. "It just seems very surprising that they would not have tested Eric, but for some reason, they didn't.

"It's so heartbreaking that it was somebody so close. I'm so sorry. I'm so sorry it's someone on Adriane's list."

Cathy, of course, told her there was no need to apologize.

When she hung up, Arlene still felt shellshocked. There was no joy in knowing the probable killer was someone married to a dear friend. "It feels like I just learned that Adriane had been killed," she said.

FORTY-FOUR

He Was Sitting Right Here

Those who knew Adriane and Leslie weren't the only ones flabbergasted by the news. The producers from *48 Hours* who had been working on the story were beside themselves. They had met Eric more than once. In fact, they'd had him only feet from the interview chair and never asked him to say a word, never pointed the camera at him. There was no reason they would have, but it was exasperating to know that in all the months they'd worked on the story, Eric was right under their noses and sometimes closer than that.

He had been present when Lily was interviewed on camera. He had driven Lily to the interview and had watched the whole thing, allegedly because he was concerned for Lily's mental well-being. She had told producers that Eric did not want her to do the interview, because every time she spoke of Adriane's death, she got very upset.

The way the interview was set up, Lily and correspondent Bill Lagattuta were in one room surrounded by the lights and cameras. In another room, the kitchen of a house that had been rented, the producers watched the interview progress on television monitors. There was food in the kitchen for the crew and for Lily and Eric if they needed anything to eat or drink. Abra Potkin, who is well known for her ability to read people, knew that Eric was not in favor of Lily doing the interview, and for that very reason, she made doubly sure he was comfortable. She offered him soda, coffee, water, candy, M&M's. She showed Eric where he would be sitting—right next to her—and he would be given his own monitor and headphones so he could see and hear what was going on with his wife in the other room.

When Eric was out of earshot, Abra remarked on the extremely different personalities of husband and wife to another producer who was there, Sue McHugh. "She is so gregarious, and he is so ice," Potkin said. "He was creepy.

I didn't think he was the killer, but I wondered how did they [Eric and Lily] connect? What did she see in him? She was robust and smiley and lively, and he was lean and put nothing out there."

Potkin is a gregarious, personable, beautiful woman whose forte is her ability to persuade people—particularly men—to do interviews they are uncomfortable with. Her way has won over countless families of murder victims, murderers, and celebrities over the years and has a tenacity that is legendary in the business. Potkin has since left *48 Hours* to become a vice president at CBS Paramount. Perhaps it's an apocryphal story, but legend has it that she was making calls for the program—still trying to nail down an exclusive interview—as she was being wheeled into labor with her second child.

When Eric seemed immune to Potkin's entreaties, it said a lot more about him than about her. Lily was emotional during the interview, talking about her dear friend who had been killed. She had to stop a few times because she was feeling overwhelmed, and each time she did, Eric tried to persuade her to leave, which didn't exactly endear him to the production crew.

Lily held fast, but it was touch and go, and the producers knew it. Potkin tried to do everything she could to reassure Eric that having Lily continue with the interview was best for everyone. When Lily started talking about her wedding day, Potkin reached over and touched Eric's arm. He pulled away. Potkin admits being shocked. "That was weird," she said. "I thought, 'What is up with this guy?' There was nothing you could do to penetrate him, not even just a little. I remember feeling there was something wrong with this guy. I can warm anyone up, and if I can't warm you up, you can't be warmed up."

Eric could not be warmed up.

Producer Sue McHugh was in the room also and had a similar reaction. In fact, later on, after Eric had come forward to say he'd been involved in Adriane's murder, McHugh thought back to that summer night when she'd gone to a baseball game with Arlene. They had run into Lily and Eric and Lily's parents, and thinking back, McHugh remembered all of them chatting excitedly about the game and the coincidence of running into each other in the parking lot. It was a happy moment, and everyone was involved in the conversation—except for Eric.

"He was loping along beside us, near the curb, not talking at all," McHugh said.

It registered on a subconscious level, but she didn't think much of it. She'd been present for Lily's interview as well and had sat next to Potkin, who was sitting next to Eric. Eric was not friendly at all, but McHugh knew from experience that there are many people who dislike the media intensely, and she put him in that category. She figured Eric and Lily had argued about Lily doing the interview—Lily had told the producers that Eric was against it—and him keeping his distance seemed normal in that context. Now that McHugh knew Eric had confessed, everything, of course, was seen in a different light.

The things Lily had said in that interview room ran through their minds: Lily had said that she hoped her friend Adriane had hurt her killer. She wondered how the killer could carry on in society and live with himself. She wondered how it was that no one close to him could realize something was wrong. Now she had the answers to all those questions. Not only did she know the killer, she was sleeping with him.

As for Potkin and McHugh, they have met plenty of killers in their day, but this was the first time either producer remembered meeting an alleged killer *before* he had been arrested.

FORTY-FIVE

Why?

The day after the arrest, Napa Police Chief Rich Melton held a massive press conference at City Hall. The story of the murders always had been a hot ticket around the Bay Area and had drawn national interest as well, so television cameras and print and radio reporters turned out in force to hear the shocking resolution to the case. There were still many questions to be answered; not the least of them was why Eric had slipped through the cracks. The police had emphasized from the very beginning of the investigation that they would start interviewing those within the small circle of friends who knew Adriane and Leslie best and then work their way out. Why would they leave Eric out of that equation? Eric was married to one of Adriane's best friends and had been inside the house on Dorset Street at least once and probably more than that. Why had it taken eleven months to interview him and ask for his DNA? Was there a rational reason for that? Was it an oversight?

Chief Melton began by thanking the families of the dead women. "They have been very helpful. They've been there for us. It's been a very difficult time for them and I can't tell you what it's like to have that kind of support from people that want answers to questions and them knowing that we have to put the investigation first. So I appreciate that very much."

Melton said the investigation had taken his men to eight different states, where they conducted more than 1,300 interviews and collected some 218 DNA samples. But it all came down to "admissions" made by Eric Copple the previous day.

Melton put the best spin he could on how Eric came to the attention of police. He said nothing about Lauren Meanza's tip and instead merely said that Eric came in because he knew "we were looking for him."

"It's my belief," the chief said, "that Eric Matthew Copple believed he was about to be caught. He made admissions that lead us to believe that he is the person that committed this crime. At approximately 3:00 a.m. on September 28, Eric Matthew Copple was booked into the Napa County detention center on two counts of murder."

District Attorney Gary Lieberstein spoke briefly and told the media that Eric was being charged with the "special circumstances of committing two murders during the same time period." He was facing twenty-six years to life for each of the two counts of murder, and if the jury agreed with Lieberstein's assessment of special circumstances, then the penalty would be life without the possibility of parole, or death. There was no bail and no murder weapon.

Chief Melton opened the floor to questions and quickly agreed that based on what Eric had told police, "you can construe that as a confession." He would not answer questions relating to motive or which of the women was targeted by Eric, only that the murders were a targeted attack.

When pressed on how the cops focused on Eric to begin with, Melton made no mention of Lauren and instead reserved credit for his own men. "As we started to get to the outer rings of relationships, if you will, that's where Eric Matthew Copple was."

Melton also said, and this was probably true, that the public release of the type of cigarettes found at the scene and linked to the killer was bound to flush out someone if that person were still in the community, as Eric was. "People that smoke know what other smokers smoke that they associate with," he said.

Overall, Melton's explanation that Eric was in the "outer ring" of the dead women's relationships struck some members of the media as specious. Eric, after all, was married to Adriane's best friend and had been in the murder house. If that did not put him close to the inner circle, what would? Furthermore, of those who were interviewed by police and who provided their DNA samples, some were clearly much more removed than Eric. The police, for instance, had taken DNA from the brother of one of Adriane's boyfriends, as well as the person who eventually bought the house on Dorset Street for slightly more than a half-million dollars. Their connections to the murders were tenuous at best, certainly further removed than Eric's. And how exactly did the police manage to collect 218 samples from men near and far but neglect someone right under their noses? And after they had Eric's name, why did they make only two calls three weeks apart? Why didn't they visit his house at night? They had traveled all over the United States but had overlooked someone in their backyard.

The Napa police really don't have an answer for those questions other than to suggest that Eric felt the ring tightening around him, felt the pressure they were exerting, and came in. More than likely, Eric's shadowy personality and his penchant for being barely there allowed him to remain hidden in plain sight. Until Lauren mentioned his name, he'd gone unnoticed for nearly a year.

But perhaps it's unfair to criticize the police too harshly. They did, after all, get a confession from Eric and apparently solved the crime. Furthermore, Eric apparently did not commit any more murders while at large for eleven months.

The person who seemed to have suffered the most as a result of his continued freedom was Lily Prudhomme, his wife of seven months. But she wasn't the only one. The families of Adriane and Leslie suffered as well; they had to live through almost a year of wondering when or if their daughters' killer would be caught. Lauren was forced to live in fear all those months, wondering if the killer would return to erase the only living witness. And finally, there were the residents of Napa Valley who had been living in fear, not knowing when the killer might strike again.

Jeff Troendly later explained that on September 1, 2005, the police had come to a turning point in their investigation. An investigative team that had begun with fifty men was basically down to two. "We had done more than 800 interviews at that point, and we were at a stalemate," Troendly said. "We had nothing."

It was time to shake things up. Detective Shulman, who'd been with the case from the beginning, was named the new lead investigator, and the focus was shifting from Leslie back to Adriane. "Leslie had tied us up for a long time," he said. "We were beginning to look at all the people on Adriane's side, and Eric was on our list. We had already visited his home and called him and called his wife. I think he knew we were on his trail."

As for whether or not Lily had any knowledge of her husband's alleged involvement with the murders, Melton said "she did not know until he approached or had been confronted about this."

Shedding a bit more light on that, Melton said that Eric was confronted by members of his own family who had seen some of his "writings."

"I believe that he felt like he was about be caught," Melton said. "And I think at that point, he revealed some of that information to family members."

When the police and DAs finished answering questions at the press conference, Arlene Allen, who was standing by the entire time, asked if she could speak to the media. Needless to say, everyone said yes immediately.

As always, Arlene was eloquent and dignified. "Thank you for all bearing with me today," she said. "One thing that I have really found in the last eleven months is how devastating an act like this can be to so many people. And now, with the arrest of Eric, the devastation continues to roll on. My heart goes out to Lily and her family and to Eric's family. I know these people. I'm very shocked at what has happened. I can't describe what my feelings are about that, because there are no words to articulate it.

"I've never felt he [Eric] was dangerous. I never felt any kind of a negative or dangerous or sinister vibe from him at all. I'm surprised at myself at this moment. I'm not feeling anger. Bitterness. Hatred. I'm not. I'm in shock, basically."

The media is infamous for asking impertinent, annoying questions, especially of families of victims, and it was no different on this day when a reporter asked Arlene, "Could you describe this horrible loss?"

Some would have told the questioner that she'd answered that far too many times to do it again, but Arlene is a kind woman. She gave an answer from her heart that was electric and had eyes tearing all over the room. "There are no words," she began, "to describe the loss that I feel. I am the mother of three daughters. Adriane was the middle daughter. We were very close. We looked alike. We were similar in personality. She lived in the area, and so therefore we had a very close relationship, and I refer to her as my significant other. As a single mom, Adriane was really the person that I longed to speak to. Felt joy whenever I saw her face. Really was anxious to see her and spend time with her. I feel in this regard that I did not only lose my beloved daughter. I lost a whole part of my own life that now leaves me kind of at a loss. I don't know how to restructure my life. I don't know what steps to take. I do know there will come a time when I will know the direction I want to take with my life, and I'll move forward, and I'll have a happy and fulfilling life, but right now I'm trying to deal with the loss of the person who was an integral part of me."

A dignified silence followed until someone else asked, "If you could say something to Eric, what would you say?"

"I think if I were to speak to Eric, I think my burning question is why. Why? What is it that makes someone feel that whatever conflict there is that the solution is to take a life? That is my big question."

FORTY-SIX

A Jealous Guy?

The best answer to the question posed by Arlene—why did Eric kill?—did not come from the police or the district attorney but from *Sentinel* publisher Harry Martin. After Eric's arrest, Martin wrote a story alleging that Eric had written a suicide note just a few days prior to his arrest, and that Eric's brother found that note and persuaded Eric to turn himself in. A friend of the family who wishes to remain unnamed said that it was the friend's understanding that the letter was mailed to Eric's brother in a nearby town but that it arrived before Eric went ahead with his planned suicide. Commander Troendly later confirmed that this was indeed what had occurred. Eric had mailed out not one but several letters, to his brother and his employers, among others. He told them that he had a dark side "that no one knows about" and that he could no longer live with himself. He did not, however, make any attempt to kill himself, which to Troendly means he was never serious about suicide. "In my experience, the people who mean to kill themselves write the note and do it then and there," Troendly said.

But at the press conference, when pointedly asked whether Eric had written a suicide note, Chief Melton hedged. He would not confirm or deny the existence of a suicide note but would only say that the cops had confiscated "writings" that belonged to Eric.

What do those writings say?

According to Martin's front-page story, Eric wrote that he had killed Adriane and Leslie because he was jealous of the close relationship between Adriane and his wife (then girlfriend), Lily. It's a crazy reason to kill someone, but murder is never rational, and in retrospect, it's easy to see how and why Eric might have felt that way. This is in no way meant to excuse his actions, but if that was the reason he carried out the murders, perhaps we have to put ourselves in his shoes and see events as he saw them.

To begin with, there is the timing of the murders. Lily and Eric originally were supposed to be married on November 1, 2004, in Hawaii, but there had been some type of argument between the couple the previous summer, and the wedding had been called off. They had even broken up for about a week. "Lily was very upset when the wedding was called off," said Ben Katz, a close friend of both Adriane and Lily. "Adriane never talked about Eric to me, but Adriane was very opinionated, and if she didn't like Eric for Lily, she would have said something."

Those who knew Adriane well agree with Ben's assessment. "Adriane could be brutally honest," said Amanda Vaughan, Adriane's childhood friend. "She was definitely someone who would speak her mind, and I got the impression she thought Lily could do better."

And there was a possibility that Adriane and Eric did not like each other, Amanda said. Before Adriane moved in with Lauren, Adriane had talked to Lily about the two of them moving in together but it never happened. "Adriane and Lily wanted to live together," Amanda said, "but Eric wanted to live with Lily, so it never happened."

Then there was the long-anticipated trip

that Adriane and Lily were to take to Australia beginning on November 25, 2004, some three weeks after the murders. Eric was not a part of that. If the wedding had taken place as planned on November 1, Eric and Lily would have been returning from their honeymoon around then. So not only was Eric not going on his honeymoon, but the only girlfriend he ever had was leaving for a long vacation halfway around the world without him. Adriane would in effect be taking his place, and one can only imagine how that would be perceived by an irrational mind.

We know from others and from what he told the police that Eric was very drunk on Halloween night. He said something to embarrass Lily, but except for those at the party, no one knows what that was. Whatever it was, Lily was upset. Later, she drove Eric to their apartment and left him there, preferring to be alone at her parents' house rather than with him. If she was that angry, is it too much to suppose that she said something to him that pressed one of his buttons? Might she have told him she was glad they were not married and glad she was going to Australia with Adriane rather than to Hawaii with him?

Did anything like this happen or not? Lily

would not talk to this author about anything related to the case.

Would that be enough to push Eric over the edge? Eric had never been arrested, did not have so much as a single traffic ticket, and, according to one person who knows him, "led a completely uninteresting life." His background argues against him having such an outsized violent reaction, except . . . Except that Eric seems to be the quintessential loner whose whole life was wrapped up in Lily, whom he met when he was a senior in high school. "Basically, Lily was his world," said Amanda Vaughan, who got all her information about Eric from Adriane. "He was not close to other people."

Arlene Allen has thought a lot about her daughter's murder and the reason Eric did what he did. "Eric was extremely controlling. He wanted to be in control over everything in his life," she said. Sometimes, Arlene said, Lily and Adriane would play with Eric by moving some household item that he had placed just so. "He didn't say anything but he made sure to move it back," Arlene said.

"He had a jealous mind," she said. She believes that, if Eric felt he were losing control—and surely he felt that way Halloween night—it might be enough to cause him to lash out.

In killing Adriane, one thing's for sure—Eric got what he wanted. Adriane was out of the picture, Lily rushed to marry him, and she never did go to Australia, so in his mind, everything worked out just fine.

FORTY-SEVEN

Under the Radar

Who is Eric Copple, really? What is he like, this alleged killer who was hiding in plain sight for eleven months? In retrospect, maybe it was not that difficult for him to fly under the radar, because if there was one thing everyone said about Eric, it was that he was quiet and unassuming. Everyone knew that he and Lily were polar opposites. "Lily was expressive and energetic, and Eric was not," said Ben Katz. "You don't even imagine this guy would want to put out that kind of energy [to kill someone]."

Ben—who'd been to Lily and Eric's wedding, watched them walk down the aisle and later celebrated with them—did not even recognize Eric's name when he first read who had been arrested for murdering Adriane. "I kept looking at the name. Eric Copple. Why does that sound so familiar? I just kept reading, and then, all of sudden, it clicked. I was just as shocked to read his name as I was when I found that Adriane was murdered. I didn't want it to be true.

"Lily's a great person, and for her to have to go through Adriane's murder, for her to confide in her boyfriend who just became her husband and probably talked about this every single day. For her to find out *this,* I feel for her so much. It makes me angry and confused, and there's just too much going on in my mind even just to think clearly about the whole thing."

Ben liked very Lily very much and was part of the tight circle of friends, along with Adriane, who often hung out together socially. Because of his friendship with Lily, he'd also met and gone out drinking with Eric on a number of occasions. As much as anyone outside of Eric's immediate family, Ben probably knew him as well as anyone, and he didn't know him at all. "Eric was shy," Ben said. "Whenever he was with Lily, she would do all the talking and he would just kind of be there with her. He wasn't distant, he was just there, and he wouldn't say much. He just seemed uncomfortable speaking."

John Brockett lived next to Eric and Lily for

two years before they moved to a new apartment after their marriage. Brockett said he had almost no contact with Eric in those two years. "He was never sociable at all," Brockett told the *Napa Valley Register*. "He never talked to me unless I talked to him. He was an odd duck."

Eric's father, Howard, was in the military, and the family moved around a lot before coming to Napa in 1996 when the elder Copple got a job with the Napa Valley State Hospital. Eric began attending Vintage High School and met Lily. Friends said he wanted to go to West Point; newspaper reports claim he did not get in but Commander Troendly said that he heard Eric *did* get in. "He got a politician to write a letter for him, but he didn't go," Troendly said. "I'm not quite sure why."

Neighbors recalled that Eric had some type of workshop in his garage where he would spend hours each night. They often could hear his saw and that might explain why, if Eric did have cuts on his hands from the murders, it would not be considered unusual.

Ben vividly remembered one of Adriane's birthday parties, where the group had a room reserved in the back of a bar. The friends were all drinking and carrying on, joking with one another and having a great time. "And at one point, Eric gets up and he just kind of stands against the wall and kind of secludes himself from the rest of the group. He doesn't want to leave or anything, because a couple of people got up and talked to him and he talked back. It was kind of weird that he was just standing there alone by himself, but Lily seemed okay with it."

It was certainly odd behavior and registered as such even at the time, but Ben said it didn't seem too odd because he knew that Eric was very shy. "If Adriane got up and stood against the wall and didn't want to talk to anybody, that to me would seem very strange but because he did it, it didn't seem as strange," Ben said.

Ben did remember Eric being most normal the day he helped move Adriane into the Dorset Street home and then at his own wedding. "He was just very normal," he said. "I was sitting with Arlene, and he came over and said hello and just seemed very normal."

Ben also said that he knew from Lily and Adriane that Eric was a "neat freak" and compulsive but never thought much of it. One time, when Adriane was living across the street from Lily and Eric, Eric thought her lawn needed to be mowed and did it himself. It's hard to make anything of that; under different circumstances, you might tell the same story and describe Eric as a thoughtful neighbor.

If there's one thing Ben could not fathom, it was how Eric could have gone through with the wedding knowing he had done what he is alleged to have done. "That must have been really stressful," Ben said. "Must have been intense. But remembering him at the wedding, I didn't notice him being upset. It just seemed like another guy getting married. He had his family with him, and everyone just seemed very happy."

Ben does remember that Eric did not dance to the song played in Adriane's honor. "I don't know why, but it didn't seem odd to me at the time. It always seemed to me that Adriane was more Lily's friend. I did not see Eric and Lily as equal friends to Adriane," he said.

And then there was the candlelight vigil Lily had organized for Adriane. What must it have been like for Eric to be so close to the center of all that mourning when he apparently was responsible? "In essence," Ben said, "he created that moment."

Even the thought of Eric being the killer never entered Ben's mind, maybe because Eric was someone who more or less blended into the wallpaper. He was, to paraphrase true crime writer

Ann Rule, the stranger living beside them. "I never felt uncomfortable while he was around," Ben continued. "Nothing stood out as being strange or odd. He didn't seclude himself entirely. He was in on the jokes, you know? He smiled. He laughed. He didn't talk much. It wasn't like, why is this guy here? He was there. He was with everybody."

FORTY-EIGHT

Halloween Night

Those who desperately wanted to hear Eric's side of the story—namely, nearly everyone in and around Napa—had to wait for months before it was revealed publicly.

The story of what Eric Copple did on the night of the Halloween murders comes directly from the testimony of Detective Todd Shulman at a preliminary hearing held in the Napa County Courthouse on October 15, 2005. In the courtroom that day were the three women inexorably linked to the murders: Arlene Allen, Cathy Harrington, and Lily Prudhomme. Eric's mother was there, as well as Lily's parents. Eric, a thin man with wire-rimmed glasses and a goatee, stood behind a bulletproof glass partition that separates the inmates from the judge, lawyers, and everyone else in this thoroughly modern courtroom. The glass, a security precaution, has the effect of making the inmates on the other side look as though they're on display. Eric, who has appeared in court with a full head of hair and completely shaved, had a full head of hair on this day. He looked curiously around the courtroom as he was led in, sometimes glancing over to his wife, Lily, and his mother, Robin. Arlene and Cathy, bonded forever as the mothers of daughters killed in the same incident, sat on the opposite side of the courtroom, Arlene holding a photo of Adriane.

It was a moment of high drama. Those in the courtroom were quiet but anxious with apprehension. They were about to hear for the first time the details of Eric's alleged confession, what the alleged killer said went on inside the Dorset Street house that Halloween night. It was emotional even for the normally unemotional Eric, who several times wiped tears from his eyes. What follows is the scenario presented by Eric to the police in the early morning hours of September 27, 2005. It should be noted that parts of his story conflict with known physical evidence. He does not, for instance, admit being in the rear of the house, where one of his cigarette butts was found.

This is Eric's story, as he remembered it:

On the evening of Halloween, 2004, Eric and Lily are at the home of friends where three couples play cards. Whoever loses a particular game has to take a drink, and Eric tells the police that he loses "quite a bit." Eric, who admits to being liquored up before going to the party, loses more than his fair share and becomes very drunk on beer and wine, so drunk that at some point he says something that embarrasses Lily. She gets upset, so upset that, at the end of the party, she drives him to the apartment they both share and leaves him there. She spends the night at her parents' home. She is house-sitting and her parents are in Hawaii, where she and Eric would have been if they'd gotten married that day as planned. If she does say anything vindictive to him, Eric does not admit it. He says he is so drunk he can't even remember Lily driving him home.

"He blacked out or passed out," Shulman said, "and at some point he woke up and went into the garage of the residence and obtained the zip ties from the garage. He also obtained a knife with a four or five inch blade. He thought it was from the garage as well. He said he then remembered driving in his vehicle and he next remembered pulling up on Dorset Street parking under a street light. He then remembered standing by the front garage of the residence on Dorset Street under a security light."

Eric's story has many black holes in it. He cannot or at least says he cannot explain why he took the zip ties with him.

Eric stands near the garage and under that security light for a long time, long enough to smoke one of his Camel Turkish Golds down to its filter. He remembers the security light going on and off with each of his movements. He moves to his right, where there is a small window to the left of the front door as one faces the house. The ledge of the window is only about three feet off the ground. He pulls his knife out and pries the window open. It is not locked and opens easily.

Eric is now in the living room. It is pitch black but he can hear a dog's low growling. It's coming from Lauren's back bedroom. He doesn't stop but moves to his right to the staircase and walks upstairs to where Adriane and Leslie are sleeping. He walks into a bedroom, and falls asleep on a pile of clothes. The next thing he remembers is a light being turned on. He jumps on the bed, not wanting the sleeping woman to make any noise.

Eric told Detective Shulman that he cannot remember everything and at this point, he said he suffered a blackout. All he recalls is being hit in the face by Adriane. If he did stab Adriane, he claims not to remember doing so. He does admit to being "panicked" when making eye contact with Adriane.

The next thing he remembers is hearing a sound behind him, some type of thud and he turns in the direction of Leslie's bedroom. Her door is open and it's very dark. Eric cannot see anyone. He closed his eyes and said he cannot recall attacking Leslie. "He said he only had partial memory of what happened," Shulman said. "Bits and pieces of different events. Flashes of memory, he called it."

After his confrontation with the women, Eric runs back down the stairs and slams his left hand on the wall. He probably knocks over a glass light at that point and cuts himself but does not recall that. He remembers climbing out the ground-floor window he used to climb into the house and remembers catching his right hand on the mini blinds as he falls outside the house. (It should be noted that the front door is directly next to the window and there is no reason for him to leave the same way he came in.)

Eric then climbs back into his car, which is parked across the street. Before getting in, he throws his knife through the open driver's side window into the car. Then, he said, he drives home. (The car must have been bloody but cops have not revealed if they found any of Adriane or Leslie's blood traces inside.) When he arrives home, he goes right to the backyard and builds a fire in an outdoor fire pit. He takes off his sweatshirt, jeans, and shoes, and burns everything. He didn't tell cops what he did with the knife.

The fact that Eric told the cops he burned his clothes but cannot remember the murders seems to indicate he may be telling the truth. After all, if he's lying about the blackouts, why not include a blackout about burning the clothes? By admitting to that, Eric just killed any chance he had for an insanity defense. Obviously, he knew what he did was wrong or why burn the bloody clothing?

The interview with Eric was videotaped and lasted between five and six hours. He was allowed to go to the bathroom, smoke a cigarette, and was given pizza and a soda.

There were some obvious holes in Eric's story that Chief Deputy District Attorney Mark Boessenecker rushed to fill in.

"Did the defendant tell you who had killed Leslie Mazzara?"

"Yes," Shulman answered.

"What did he say?"

"He said he did."

Boessenecker bored in. "Did the defendant tell you who had killed Adriane Insogna?"

"Yes."

"What did he say?"

"He said he did."

Later, the prosecutor asked the question in a different way. "Did he describe for you him stabbing Adriane?"

"He couldn't describe the details of the stabbing," Shulman testified.

"Yet he acknowledged that he had killed both these young women, is that correct?"

"Yes."

"What was his demeanor, the defendant's demeanor, during the course of the interview?"

"I would describe it as very collected, very deliberate in his answers. He paused before answering to think about what he wanted to say."

"As part of that contact with the defendant that night, did you also take a DNA sample from him?"

"Yes."

Eric's lawyer, Deputy Public Defender Greg Galeste, followed up with some questions of his own for Shulman.

"And at any time during the interview that you conducted with him, did he appear at all to be depressed?" Galeste asked.

"Yes," Shulman answered. "He was expressing to me problems in his family and the problems in his life that year that he felt contributed to what happened."

"Did he appear to be sad?"

"When talking about his issues in his family, yes, in his life."

"Was he tearful at all?"

"Not when I was talking to him."

It is not known exactly what family issues Eric was referring to but his parents, Howard and Robin, had filed for separation in March, 2004, after twenty-nine years of marriage, and they officially filed for divorce in May, 2006. "[Eric] said there was some depression that he had in 2004 before this happened because of some family issues and that he had also felt depressed about what he did afterward and had been suicidal after realizing he had done this," Shulman told the court.

Boessenecker ended the hearing by introducing the death certificates of Adriane and Leslie, which showed that the causes of death for both women were multiple stab wounds. Most important, though, Boessenecker revealed that Eric's DNA was found on the rubber band holding the zip ties together, on the section of wall board removed from the house that was near the bottom of the stairs, from the bloodstains on the window blinds, and from the saliva on both cigarette butts found outside the house.

It seemed like a rock-solid case. The only hope for Eric appeared to be a defense of diminished capacity or impaired judgment because he allegedly was drunk. His lawyers will point to the absence of any type of trouble with the law before this and argue that was an extraordinary event in the life of a rather ordinary, law-abiding citizen.

Of course, DA Boessenecker anticipated that at the prelim and made an impassioned plea before Judge Stephen Kroyer, laying out the reasons that Eric knew exactly what he was doing. Boessenecker's soliloquy sounded very much like a mini-closing argument and was intended to allow Eric and his lawyers very little wiggle room.

"Your honor," the DA began, "I think that one thing that's very evident from the evidence that's been presented today is that, while the defendant's acknowledged his responsibility for taking the lives of Adriane Insogna and Leslie Mazzara, the spin he puts on the killings is frankly contradicted by the physical evidence.

"The evidence demonstrates that, in the dead of night—this didn't happen in broad daylight but in the dead of night—he got into a car, operated that car, drove across town to a predetermined location. He went there prepared. He brought with him two specific items to assist him in committing this crime. He brought flex ties which can be used for binding, and he brought a knife.

"When he got to the house, instead of staggering around in some kind of drunken stupor, as his statement to Detective Shulman would suggest, what we find out is he took some time waiting and watching and determining what was the best time to enter and what was the best way to enter.

"Physical evidence of the cigarette butts tells us that he went in the rear of the house to case out the house, and he went into the front of the house to figure out the best location to enter. He was looking for the right spot to enter. He was looking for the right time to enter.

"He got into that house through the window, and he did so without drawing much attention at all from the women that were living in that house. He got up the stairs without so much as any indication to the one roommate who was downstairs that he was doing that. Again, completely inconsistent with someone in some kind of alcoholic blackout. He goes so quietly to cause little concern to his victims.

"And then when he gets upstairs, he savagely, brutally, and viciously exterminates their young lives and then he is out of the house. He's undetected. He's not caught. He gets rid of evidence.

"I think the evidence that has been presented here clearly shows that he should be held for two counts of murder with the special allegations, as well as the special circumstances of multiple murder. Thank you."

Judge Kroyer agreed there was probable cause. The Napa district attorney has not yet said whether he will seek the death penalty, although by asking for two counts of murder with special circumstances, he is headed that way.

FORTY-NINE

The Enduring Mystery

To this day, the mystery at the heart of this case is still the question of motive. If Eric did kill Adriane and Leslie as he allegedly said he did, why did he do it? Could his raging jealousy of Adriane and Lily's relationship truly be the root cause? It doesn't make any logical sense, of course, but it's impossible to see things as a drunken Eric Copple did that Halloween night. He was drunk, his girlfriend was mad at him, he was sitting at home alone on the night that was to have been his wedding night, and his girlfriend was about to take off on a fun vacation without him. Sure, it's depressing, but 99.9 percent of the population would have slept it off. But it's impossible to rationalize an irrational act.

Another possibility is that Eric had a thing for Leslie, as many men did. There is a rumor circulating that Eric was infatuated with Leslie, and once refused to leave the house with Lily so he could continue talking to Leslie. Did Eric make a pass at Leslie, and was he afraid she would tell Lily? Did Eric make a pass at Adriane and was afraid she would tell Lily? And what exactly was the reason for those zip ties he carried to the house with him?

"We may never know the real reason," Commander Troendly said. "I don't believe the reason he gave us." Troendly would not elaborate, but we know from the preliminary hearing that Eric said he was having some unnamed "family problems."

Cathy Harrington said that murder is a senseless crime, and she's right. Most likely, only Eric Copple knows why he did what he did, and, if he blacked out as he claims, maybe even he doesn't know. It's possible that Lily has the best handle on what happened, but she's not talking to the press. One wonders what it was that Eric said at the party that embarrassed her, and what she said in response. The murders of these two women will never make sense, but knowing about that conversation between Lily and Eric will likely clear it up a bit.

FIFTY

After

A year to the day after finding out her daughter had been murdered, Arlene Allen kept a promise to herself and climbed once again to the top of the Sydney Harbor Bridge to look down at wondrous Sydney Harbor and take in the sights her middle daughter will never see. She recalled the first time there, feeling Adriane's spirit. She felt it once again this time, but she doubts she'll ever climb up there again. The memory is just too painful. On the positive side, Arlene is getting on with her life the best she can, having taken a new job as the office manager and accountant for a local grocery store in Calistoga.

Cathy Harrington remains a minister in Ludington, Michigan. On August 1, 2005, the day

Leslie would have turned twenty-seven—Cathy took a five-day kayaking trip and spiritual retreat on Lake Superior. She said she suffered post traumatic stress following Leslie's murder and began two-hour grief counseling sessions in Traverse City, which she continued into the summer of 2006. In August 2006, Cathy flew to South Carolina on what would have been Leslie's twenty-eighth birthday to have dinner with her sons PJ and Andy and Leslie's friends Kelly McCorkle and Amy Brown. They spent Leslie's birthday together, remembering how special she was to all of them.

Kelly, now married, continues to organize and plan the Raising Race to raise money for a cottage to be built in Leslie's name. Groundbreaking on the Leslie Mazzara Cottage took place on August 24, 2006. The final cost will be $250,000, but Kelly is determined to make it happen, and those who know her say the cottage is a foregone conclusion.

I would be less than honest if I did not share Cathy's abhorrence concerning the media's treatment of her daughter's memory. Cathy feels victimized by the way media handled and covered her daughter's death, cringing at the way Leslie was referred to as a beauty queen over and over, as though there were nothing more to her life than that. But more than that, Cathy wishes overall that the entertainment industry would stop glorifying violence. In one of our lengthy e-mail exchanges, she quoted from an essay by Holocaust survivor Elie Wiesel: "Listen to survivors and respect their wounded sensibility. Open yourselves to their scarred memories and stop insulting the dead."

Leslie's father, Lenny, who remains in prison, feels a different set of emotions. In a letter he wrote to this author, he said, "Not a day goes by without having thoughts of Leslie, and at the end, there is always a smile on my face as to the recent memories of her. I cannot take any credit for her upbringing, but that does not diminish how proud she made me feel to be her dad."

Amy Brown is married and happy—as happy as she can be without Leslie. "I don't know," she said, "if I'll ever be able to say, 'My best friend is no longer here because she was stabbed to death.' It doesn't sound real when I'm talking about it right now."

At the Niebaum-Coppola winery, there is a small vineyard next to the main estate house. The vineyard is maintained by employees and it has been renamed for Leslie Mazzara. Those grapes have yet to be harvested, but given Leslie's sunny personality, the staff is confident one day they will savor the special wine. Kelly, for one, appreciates the gesture. "It's very meaningful to me and her family because it is something that represents life," Kelly said. "The wine production is just going to keep going and going and never stop. Having the vineyard there keeps her memory alive, and it's never going to die. It's going to be there. I can come back and visit Niebaum-Coppola when I'm sixty-five with my grandkids, and it'll still be there. So, in a way, Leslie is going to outlive us all."

The police have not said who was sending Leslie the envelopes full of cash, and that may remain a secret forever.

It might seem odd to some, but two of those closest to Adriane, her mother, Arlene, and her best buddy, Ben, are still in touch with Lily as *she* now goes through the most painful ordeal of her life—being married to the man accused of murdering her best friend. "Arlene's so selfless," said Ben Katz. "Arlene has said very precious things about Lily and how she doesn't think Eric's a monster."

For her part, Arlene is not revealing any confidences. She will just say that she and Lily have talked, and it's evident in court that there is no outward animosity. When she and Lily see each other in the courtroom hallways during the preliminary hearings, there is an imperceptible nod by both women. Sometimes, Arlene even sits in a row just behind Lily on the same side of the courtroom.

Lily usually stays close to her parents and Eric's mother, who comes to the proceedings with her pastor. Arlene has started bringing a number of friends to the hearings. She had been coming by herself but felt that, since Lily was coming with an "entourage," as she put it, she would bring one herself. Arlene surrounds herself with good buddy Lauren and other close friends. What's tragically clear is that Lily herself would be part of Arlene's group if not for the situation she finds herself in.

Both Arlene and Ben are nonplussed that Lily is standing by Eric, at least so far. People wonder if eventually she'll divorce him but, for now, she is living up to her wedding vows and standing by her man in exceedingly bad times.

Soon after Eric was arrested, Lily sent an e-mail to Ben, who said "she was apologizing and she was kind of just describing how confused she was. She was very upset, and after I read her e-mail, I called her and talked to her."

Ben, who is very kind and loyal, said the last

thing he wanted to do was ask Lily about the case. That was not, he said, why he got in touch with her. "What I was trying to do as I was talking to her was just make things a little more normal. I knew she was reading the latest Harry Potter book just before Eric was arrested, so I asked her if she'd finished it yet. She laughed a little bit, and it felt so good to hear her be able to laugh, because her e-mail was so heavy and I was thinking that what she was going through was very heavy. The laugh, small as it was, was genuine.

"It must have felt good to her because she opened up and at the end of the conversation, she said, 'If you ever wanna talk, just call.' And I told her the same thing but it's easier to talk to her by e-mail because it's still emotional for me."

Lily still works in the Napa Sanitation District, where her best friend Adriane used to work. In light of the murders and the arrest of the husband of one of its well-liked employees, it must be a very sobering place to work. One imagines that none of the fifty or so employees ever mentions Eric Copple or Adriane Insogna, at least not while Lily is present. Those who work there want to see Eric pay for what he allegedly did to Adriane and Leslie, even while they feel great sympathy for Lily.

As for Lily, it's unknown what she thinks.

She's moved in with her mother and holds herself with dignity in court, looking straight ahead and exchanging not a word with anyone besides her parents and Eric's parents. She does visit Eric regularly in the Napa County detention center and these days calls herself Lily Prudhomme-Copple.

The situation makes for some very curious talk, and the big question is whether or not Lily knew that Eric was involved long before he turned himself in. How could she not know when she lived with him every day and slept with him every night? Did she not see scratches on him? Did she not ask him where he was the night of the murders?

Ben Katz dismisses that talk as ridiculous. "When I talked to Lily," he said, "she seemed very shocked by it [Eric's arrest]. I could just hear it in her voice that she was very, very tired and that she just had no clue. There must be a million things going through her mind.

"Adriane's and Leslie's murders changed our lives forever, but for Lily, it's got to be devastating. I can see how she would not be able to trust anyone. I mean, this is going to change her life forever."

FIFTY-ONE

"I Admit, Your Honor"

For Napa, it was a relatively cold morning on December 5, 2006. The outside temperature was 39 degrees and car windows had frosted overnight. By 8:15 that morning, those most closely affected by the double murders of Adriane Insogna and Leslie Mazzara were making their way into the Napa County Criminal Court building at Third and Main Streets. This was to be the day of reckoning for Eric Matthew Copple, and the frosty outside air would extend all the way into the third floor courtroom of Judge Francisca Tisher.

One of the first to arrive at the courthouse was Eric's beleaguered mother Robin—perpetually red-faced as if she'd just finished crying. She kept her head down, ignoring the single cameraman aiming his camera at her. She climbed the steps along with her pastor and advisor and, as usual, said not a word. Next to arrive, from the opposite side of the courthouse, was Eric's wife, Lily. Lily had changed her physical appearance since the last court hearing. Her strawberry blond hair was darker and the curls were gone. She wore big sunglasses and looked straight ahead with her singular dignity and posture that screamed, "I've done nothing wrong." And she hasn't. She's as much a victim of Eric Copple's lies and pathology as anyone.

Next to make her way up the street was Lauren Meanza, the sole survivor in the house on Dorset Street on the night Adriane and Leslie had died. Lauren, long and lanky, had not appeared at the recent hearings on the case but, like everyone else this morning, she knew the end was near. She had since moved to Los Angeles and her very appearance here in Napa was a clear signal that, after all the continuances in the case, this hearing was for real. She was flanked on either side by her parents who had to be the most thankful people in the courthouse that day. Somehow, their daughter had been spared the unimaginable.

Peripheral lawyers made their way inside

the courthouse until, finally, from three or four blocks away, a small crowd appeared at 8:25 a.m., five minutes before the hearing was to begin. Those in the crowd did not hurry because they all-knew nothing would happen until they got upstairs. Leading the way was Napa District Attorney Gary Lieberstein and his underling Chief Deputy District Attorney Mark Boessenecker. Both men walked stiff as rods and, as usual, the thin-lipped Boessenecker looked like he had enjoyed a plate of lemons for breakfast. His face—with its wispy mustache and tight expression—was as dour as his personality. Right behind the men walked Adriane's mother, Arlene, and Leslie's mother, Cathy, who had traveled from her home in Michigan. They stood shoulder to shoulder against the morning cold surrounded by various friends and family. Cathy's sons, PJ and Andy, were not there but Lexi, Arlene's daughter and Adriane's sister, was present along with her husband. Arlene's other daughter Allison was still in Australia.

Upstairs, the proceedings had been moved to a different courtroom on the third floor. The families and friends of Adriane and Leslie sat, as usual, on the right side while Lily and her family sat on the left. But there was a difference this day. The jury box happened to be

on the left side which meant the defendant—
Eric Copple—by custom was required to sit on
the right side but no one realized that until he
walked in from a holding cell. Eric strode into
the courtroom, not making eye contact with
anyone. His hair was cut short and he still had
his trademark crewcut, wire-rim glasses, and
goatee. He did look more put together but that
was simply a function of what he was wearing—
a black suit, white shirt, and black tie. Gone
was his jailhouse jumpsuit, another sign that
today was serious.

He sat right where the correction officers in-
structed him, at the defense table directly in front
of those supporting Adriane and Leslie. Anyone
could see the unhappiness on their faces because
they had inadvertently placed themselves on Eric's side. Sitting three rows back, Lauren Meanza
later told reporters she felt her whole body tense
up when Eric entered the courtroom.

For the next hour and a half, there were numerous conferences in chambers and sidebars
with the judge who allowed the media to sit in
the jury box so they could see and hear everything. A single CBS television cameraman and
one still cameraman from the *Napa Valley Register* were allowed in. Because the media was in
the jury box, it was easy to see Eric's comings

and goings and, each time he was escorted to the back, he was made to take off his tie and then put it back on before coming back into court. The authorities were not willing to give Eric enough rope to hang himself but they were going to make him pay for what he'd done.

Mark Boessenecker rose to address Judge Tisher and advised her that "we have a plea agreement." Then he unveiled the details:

Eric was pleading guilty to two counts of first-degree murder and admitting to all the special circumstances in the case—essentially that he laid in wait for his victims—and he waived any and all rights of appeals that he had. The district attorney agreed not to seek the death penalty. In exchange, Eric would receive a sentence of life in prison with no possibility of parole. He was never to ask for a pardon or leniency and, if he ever did, the district attorney had the right to again seek the death penalty against him.

Judge Tisher addressed Eric and asked if he had initialed every page of the plea agreement and if he understood what he was agreeing to. Eric said he did. Judge Tisher ticked off parts of the agreement. Did he use a knife to commit these murders? Did he lie in wait for his victims? Did he stab them to death?

To each, Judge Tisher asked, "Do you admit or deny?"

To each, Eric answered, "I admit, your honor."

The proceedings were clinical in light of the crimes Eric was admitting to—taking the lives of two vibrant young women in the most horrible way imaginable.

Arlene and Cathy shed a few tears but clearly seemed cried out after suffering what Eric had done more than two years earlier. They say it hurts to cry a lot and these two mothers were clearly hurting.

Sentencing was set for January 11, 2007, but that was just a formality. Everyone had just heard what the sentence was.

The question of why Eric Copple had done what he'd done hung in the air but he was not talking, nor was any member of his family. What's more, the plea agreement included a stipulation that they were never to talk to the media about his crimes or they would risk having Eric tried for the death penalty. Observers say that Napa District Attorney Gary Lieberstein very much wanted to try the case and wanted Eric to get the death penalty but his hands were tied by the families of Adriane and Leslie. Arlene Allen told friends she could not bear to go through a trial and Cathy Harrington, a woman of the cloth, was against the death penalty. With Eric pleading to everything the DA threw at him, what was the point of going to trial and spending a large amount of the county's money?

The plea also satisfied Eric's side. His mother, Robin, had told friends that she was terrified of her son receiving the death penalty. She leaned heavily on her religion and never came to the court without her pastor at her side. But her religion got her into some trouble as well. At one point, Robin sent a letter to Arlene Allen apologizing for what had happened to Adriane but she never mentioned her son or his motive. Instead, Robin wrote that the murders were "God's will." *That* did not sit well with Arlene, who let Robin know in no uncertain terms that it was all Eric's fault for allowing his rage to rise up. Rather than being God's will, Arlene wrote back that "Jesus wept at these women's deaths."

After the plea bargain, Arlene and Cathy lingered in the hallway outside the courtroom. They said all the right things about being relieved and glad there was an end to the case. Their lives were moving on—without their beloved daughters, but move on they would. Their lives would never be the same but at least the case was behind them.

FIFTY-TWO

The Final Showdown

Although Eric Copple had agreed to serve the rest of his natural life in prison without any possibility of parole, the American justice system demands that there be a formal sentencing. Copple was soon to disappear behind the thick brick walls of San Quentin forever but, before he did, the families of Adriane and Leslie were entitled to tell him exactly how they felt about what he'd done to them. January 11, 2007, was their day to confront Copple.

As they had a month before, everyone associated with the case assembled in the third floor courtroom of Judge Francisca Tisher. There were the usual procedural arguments over the media's request to videotape and photograph the proceedings. The judge issued limitations. Those who did not want to be photographed or recorded would be exempt. Leslie's family and all her friends felt stung by the way the media portrayed her and refused to allow anyone to take their picture. Arlene Allen, however, felt differently. She wanted her speech recorded for posterity, and so did Lily and Eric Copple.

The Reverend Cathy Harrington chose to speak first and she quietly read a moving thirteen-page statement filled with her memories of Leslie's life. She recounted Leslie's life from her birth to the time Cathy invited her to California. But that was only the warm-up. Cathy then angled her body slightly to address Copple but this preacher did not have forgiveness on her mind. "I'm told, Mr. Copple, that you have found God since your senseless rampage," she told him. "It is right for us to hope that sometime, somewhere down the long road ahead, you will learn to take these murders into your heart like a man and let the guilt tear and rip apart your heart from the inside out, as your senseless and violent act resulting in the murders of Leslie and Adriane have done to all who loved them and whose lives they touched.

"I know that I will navigate the rest of my life with a broken heart. As a mother and a minister, I wish I could tell you that I forgive you. At this time, I cannot."

Copple, dressed in a pin-striped suit and dark tie, did not react much at all to Cathy or to any of the victim impact statements that were delivered in quick succession, from Leslie's Grammy, her brothers PJ and Andy, and her friends Kelly McCorkle and Amy Brown. Leslie's two closest friends gave statements that were remarkably different in tone. Amy, always full of spitfire, addressed Copple the entire time and wound up her talk by telling him "May you live a hundred years in misery and an eternity in hell."

Kelly, married and pregnant, was a bundle of nerves and was visibly shaking, but she found room in her heart for Copple: "I want you to know that it is very hard to live without somebody you love so much but I forgive you."

Throughout the statements, Copple looked straight ahead and fingered his goatee. Nothing seemed to affect him, not even the blown-up photos of Leslie and the slides of Adriane and her friends, including Lily, that were projected onto a giant screen. Given what the speakers were saying, there was surprisingly little emotion in the courtroom—until, that is, the moment Arlene stood and walked to the lectern.

Arlene's face was tight and those who knew

her could read anger in her eyes. Metaphorically, she got right in Copple's face by reminding him in stark terms that Adriane was not some nameless victim and that she was not an unknown stranger. "Eric, you knew Adriane—she counted you among her friends. And you know me. Do you remember how we met?" she asked.

Copple continued to look down but his face grew redder and he sometimes rubbed at his forehead as if trying to tear off the skin. Whatever Arlene was saying, it was one giant headache to Copple.

"Eric, I know you. I know that you are a man who brutally and callously took the life of a wonderful woman . . . you are a man who violently stabbed to death the best friend of the woman you love. That is not love, Eric. You cannot love Lily and murder her best friend. You cannot love Lily and bring a knife into Adriane's home and stab her—and stab her again and again and again and again."

The words "and again" bounced off the walls of the courtroom as Arlene repeated them over and over, probably a dozen times. Her voice got louder and louder as she stared Copple down. She pounded on the lectern. No one dared move; she looked that angry. Copple looked like he'd rather be anywhere but in that chair.

Arlene rubbed Copple's face in what he'd done. She zeroed in on her daughter's slit throat, slit by the man sitting just a few feet away. At that moment, Arlene very much had her foot on Copple's throat and was pressing down hard.

"My baby never wore a turtleneck sweater in her life and yet she had to be buried in one and still it could not hide the extent of her wounds, wounds that you inflicted on her. Yes, I know you, Eric.

"You are a man who is so cruel as to invite me, the mother of the woman you murdered, to stand up for you at your wedding, to read scripture to you of love and death and to bless your union. I know you, Eric. You are a murderer and a coward. You are defined by your actions, Eric, and yours prove you to be the basest of murderers, a liar and a coward. So I say to you, Eric, go! Leave this world of family and friends, of hopes and dreams, of life and love and laughter. There is no place for you here. For while in the years ahead, the memory of Leslie and Adriane will remain clear and shining bright in our hearts and in our minds, you will be forgotten. And when that door closes behind you today, I will think of you no more."

Arlene turned and sat down. She was the final speaker to represent the victims. Copple's face was placid no more. It was as though he finally understood he was in big trouble and that people were very angry with him. Arlene had cracked his façade.

Then, Lily stood. The judge asked her to identify herself, and, with a small smile, she said Lily Copple. Her husband turned and stared at her. Her voice was filled with conviction as she thanked Adriane's and Leslie's families for agreeing to the plea bargain and sparing Copple the death penalty. She mentioned Arlene by name for continuing to be "loving and supportive" toward Lily even after learning the truth about Copple. Lily spoke of the days leading up to the moment Copple turned himself in to police. She said she knew something terrible was bothering him and begged him to tell her what it was. She said she promised him then, "Eric, there is nothing in this world you can do to make me love you less."

Her voice cracked as Eric wept and then she went further, telling him publicly, "These words are just as true today as they were on that afternoon." It was a touching and magnanimous moment for a woman whose life has been torn apart in an unimaginable way. What no one knew was that, when Copple initially told Lily he had killed Adriane, he "proved" it by showing her the scar where he cut his hand while hacking Adriane to death.

But Lily was just warming up. She was about

to "go there," to explain as best she could the reason Copple committed the murders. The pressure on Lily was surely crushing but she continued. "For those of us who know and love Eric it is still inexplicable that this fine man can be responsible for such a terrible crime," she said. "Nothing in his past gave any indication of a potential for violence. He is an exceptional student, intensely intelligent with very high standards of honesty and a strong Christian faith known for his gentleness and reserve.

"We can piece together several factors of his actions on that night: An extremely difficult family situation, a chronic severe clinical depression, and self medication with excessive amounts of alcohol all combined with a series of emotional shocks to form a perfect storm of conditions that sent Eric's normal self control into a horrific explosion. He has no recollection of motivation or planning and most of all he has done the hard work of reconciliation with God."

Finally, Lily finished her talk by telling the world, "I can say without hesitation that the man who committed this crime is not present in the person or mind of my husband today."

It was an extraordinary speech for everything it said about not only Copple but Lily too. And then, finally, it was Copple's turn.

Would he explain himself? Say he was sorry? Reveal his motive? The more those in the courtroom strained to hear what he was about to say, the more it seemed Copple could not squeeze out even one word. He continued to rub his head, harder than ever, and he literally pulled at his collar, straining for just a bit more breath. The noose around his neck was growing tighter by the moment. This was most likely the last time he'd ever appear in public and he was not yet thirty. His two lawyers, Amy Morton and Greg Galeste, patted him on his back and handed him a cup of water.

Finally, he began with the words "I am a broken man," but then stopped again and muttered, "This sucks."

It was painful but no one could turn away. He began again. "I am a broken man," he said again and then continued, "a man splintered by a penetrating awareness of my own potential for wickedness. While I cannot fathom the full extent of the anguish I have caused, I recognize that my sinful deeds have inflicted terrific agony on a great number of people. The words evade me to articulate the depths of my sorrow or the turmoil I created.

"To whatever extent I am able I will endeavor some of the circumstances that led up to this heinous crime. I have suffered from severe depression from adolescence and I had strong suicidal tendencies from my early teenage years. I always have been a decidedly introverted person.

"In the months preceding Halloween 2004, several traumatic events happened in my life in rapid succession. My immediate family dissolved largely as a result of certain disturbing revelations about specific members. My beloved grandfather experienced a debilitating stroke and passed away. Financially, I was in dire straits and could not secure meaningful employment and worst of all in my estimation my relationship with Lily—the singular ray of light in my otherwise black world—was in peril of collapsing.

"These and other factors fertilized the seed of anger sowed in my heart as a youth. Lily pleaded with me and her parents implored me to accept the help I so desperately needed. I proudly and stubbornly refused and instead turned to alcohol and stimulants. My depression only worsened."

Copple then turned toward those in attendance. "Arlene and Cathy, I am mournfully sorry for stealing Adriane and Leslie from you. I am sorry for all the horrific trauma you have endured on that black night and in all the subsequent days.

"Sorry is a pathetic little word but I know of no other word that can adequately describe what I feel. I am sorry for deceiving so many for so long, my own family included. I thought September 27, 2005 [the day he surrendered to police] would be my last day in this body, the last violence this set of hands would ever do."

Copple then took on the district attorney who had accused Copple of lying to police in his confession. Whatever else can be said about Copple, he seemed to be speaking from his heart. "In my statement to the police," he said, "I was completely honest and forthright. I told the truth and God is my witness. I am willing to do anything and everything possible to assuage the anguish of the bereaved."

And then, he was done talking and turned his chair back toward the judge. Copple had bared his soul and showed his hand. The murders were the result of depression, anger, and rage, all fueled by a lack of self-awareness and failure to seek help. He had done the unthinkable and explaining why had not made it any more palatable.

By calling Lily "the singular ray of light in my otherwise black world," and saying that he feared the relationship was in danger of collapse, Copple seemed to confirm what those closest to the case always suspected—he'd killed Adriane because he was jealous of her, jealous she might talk Lily into breaking off their relationship once and for all. Whether that was true or not, it was true for Copple. It seemed that Leslie had the misfortune to be in the wrong place at the worst possible time.

It was a raw day inside the courtroom and everyone was emotionally drained. The crowd staggered outside, into the bright sunshine of a winter afternoon. It was hard to make sense of what had happened in there, just was it was hard to make sense of the last two and a half years. Had it all really happened here, in this little tourist town that was the gateway to the wine country and the good life? From the courthouse steps, all one could see was clear blue sky in every direction. The forecast had been for rain but the sun's rays felt brighter and warmer than ever.

We were still in Napa, after all, where everything is just so beautiful.